KW-480-401

HAWAII
• AT COST •
A TRAVELLER'S GUIDE

LITTLE HILLS PRESS

© Photographs — Hawaii Visitors Bureau, Sydney
© Maps — Little Hill Press, 1990

Cover by Stuart Williams
Typeset and printed in Singapore by Singapore National Printers Ltd

© Little Hill Press, 1990
ISBN 1 86315 007 2

Little Hills Press Pty. Ltd.,
Tavistock House, 34 Bromham Road,
Bedford MK40 2QD,
United Kingdom.

Regent House,
37-43 Alexander Street,
Crows Nest NSW 2065 Australia.

Distributed in USA and Canada by
The Talman Company, Inc
150 Fifth Avenue
New York NY 10011 USA

DISCLAIMER
Whilst all care has been taken by the publisher and authors to ensure that the information is accurate and up to date, the publisher does not take responsibility for the information published herein. The recommendations are those of the editorial team and as things get better or worse, places close and others open, some elements in the book may be inaccurate when you get there. Please write and tell us about it so we can update in subsequent editions.

CONTENTS

Page

THE HAWAIIAN ISLANDS   7
(Introduction, History, Climate, Population, Language,
Religion, Festivals, Entry Regulations, Embassies,
Money, Communications, Miscellaneous)

TRAVEL INFORMATION   23
(How To Get There, Accommodation, Local Transport,
Food, Shopping, Sport and Recreation)

OAHU   27

HAWAII — THE BIG ISLAND   61

MAUI   89

MOLOKAI   111

KAUAI   121

LANAI   139

NIIHAU   145

INDEX   147

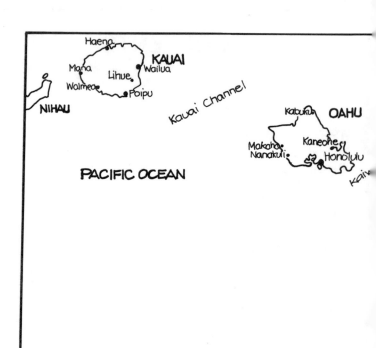

Haena
Mana
KAUAI
Lihue
Wailua
Waimea
Poipu
NIHAU
Kauai Channel
Kahuku
OAHU
Makaha
Kaneohe
Nanakuli
Honolulu
Kaiw
PACIFIC OCEAN

N

HAWAIIAN ISLANDS

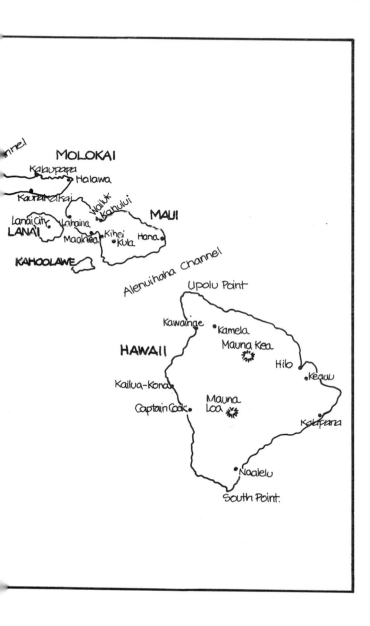

Windsurfing

THE HAWAIIAN ISLANDS

The Islands of Hawaii are situated approximately 3,870km (2,400 miles) south-west of the coast of California, 4,485km (2,781 miles) south of Alaska, 6,205km (3,847 miles) east of Tokyo, and 8,065km (5,000 miles) north-east of Sydney. The eight islands which make up the main group are the result of underwater volcanic cataclysms hundreds of thousands of years ago in the 3,226km (2,000 miles) fault at the bottom of the Pacific Ocean. Even today, Hawaii is a land in the making. Its two active volcanoes are among the most spectacular in eruption, and among the least harmful to human life in the world.

The Hawaiian archipelago stretches 2,451km (1,523 miles) south-east to north-west from Cape Kumukahi, the easternmost point of the *Island of Hawaii* (known as the Big Island), to the tiny speck known as Kure Atoll. Seven of the eight most southerly islands are the inhabited portions of the State. Three of the north-western Hawaiian Islands had a total population of 31 persons in the 1980 census.

The Big Island has a total land area of 10,407km^2 (4,034 sq miles) and a population of 111,800. It is almost twice the size of the other islands combined. The island grows sugar, coffee, cattle and macadamia nuts, and has two volcanoes, Mauna Loa and Kilauea.

Maui is the second largest with an area of 1,881km^2 (729 sq miles) and 78,700 inhabitants. The Valley Isle produces sugar and pineapple, and cattle and horses are reared there. The 3,054m (10,023 ft) Haleakala is the largest dormant volcano crater in the world. Lahaina was Hawaii's capital before 1845, and still has some of the atmosphere of an old whaling town.

Next in size is *Oahu*, 1,533km^2 (594 sq miles), the most populated island with 816,700 people. Home to the capital city of Honolulu, the principal port, the major airport, the business and financial centre, and the educational heart of the State, Oahu is probably best known for the famous Waikiki Beach, Diamond Head and Pearl Harbour.

Kauai, the Garden Island 1,416km² (549 sq miles) with 46,100 inhabitants, offers magnificent scenery and lush vegetation, waterfalls, the spectacular Waimea Canyon, the 'hidden' valley of Kalalau, and colourful tropical plants and flowers.

Next comes *Molokai* with an area of 673km² (261 sq miles) and a population of 6,700. Known as the Friendly Isle, Molokai has pineapple plantations, ranches, and some spectacular cliffs along its northern Pali Coast. On a 34km² (13 sq mile) peninsula below high cliffs is Kalaupapa, the Hansen's Disease settlement, officially called Kalawao County.

Almost the entire island of *Lanai*, 361km² (140 sq miles) with 2,200 inhabitants, is a Dole Company pineapple plantation.

Niihau is a privately owned island, with livestock raising as its principal industry. Legend says it was the original home of the goddess Pele. The area of the island is 181km² (70 sq miles) and the population, 214.

Kahoolawe is an uninhabited island used as a target by US Navy and Air Force. The 116km² (45 sq miles) is littered with unexploded shells, and no one is allowed to go ashore without permission.

There have been various explanations of the name 'Hawaii'. It is said to have been named by Hawaii Loa, traditional discoverer of the islands, after himself. Hawaii or Hawaiki, traditional home of the Polynesians, is also given as the origin. This is a compound word, Hawa, the name of the traditional place of residence, and -ii or -iki, meaning little or small, thus, a smaller or new homeland. Since -ii also means raging or furious, the name is sometimes explained as referring to the volcanoes. It is often written with the glottal-stop mark: Hawai'i.

HISTORY

It was long believed that the Polynesians first arrived in Hawaii from Tahiti around 1000 AD, but new discoveries have suggested that the true date may be closer to the 6th century AD or even earlier. Researchers believe that the Polynesians who conquered the Pacific in their double-hulled canoes came originally from South-East Asia. Tahiti is thought to be one centre of Polynesian development, but there is evidence indicating that Hawaii was first settled from the Marquesas. Regardless, to those familiar with the vast reaches of the Pacific Ocean, the seamanship of the Polynesians is a feat of staggering proportions.

The intrepid British explorer, Captain James Cook, is credited with discovering Hawaii in 1788, when he sighted Oahu and landed on Kauai. Cook named the archipelago the Sandwich Islands, after his patron the Earl of Sandwich, and for many years the islands were so known in the western world. On Sunday, February 14, 1779, Cook was slain in a fight with the Hawaiians at Kealakekua on the Island of Hawaii. Previously the islanders had thought Cook was the god Lono, who had vowed to return to his people, but they changed their minds, and proved just how mortal he was.

At the time of Cook's arrival each island was ruled as an independent kingdom by hereditary chiefs. One such chief, Kamehameha, consolidated his power on the island of Hawaii in a series of battles, about 1790, and then conquered Maui and Oahu. By the time of his death in 1819, Kamehameha I had united the islands under his rule and had established the Kingdom of Hawaii which survived until 1893.

In 1820, the first American missionaries arrived from New England. Not only did they bring Christianity to a people becoming disillusioned with their ancient gods, but they represented the first of several migrations which led to the cosmopolitan character of Hawaii's people today. With the arrival of people from distant lands, new diseases were introduced, to which the natives had no immunity. They also had no immunity to the alcohol brought by these new arrivals, and a state of chaos was soon reached. The missionaries gained great success because they aligned themselves with the chiefs against some of these evils.

Kamehameha's eldest son, Liholiho, took the title of Kamehameha II. His short reign was noted for the official demise of the old religion and the breakdown of ancient tabus. Liholiho and his queen, Kamamalu, both died of measles within a few days of each other while visiting London in 1824.

Another son of Kamehameha, Kauikeaouli, was proclaimed King with the title of Kamehameha III. During his 30-year reign, many hazards to the little kingdom were surmounted, and its independence recognised by the great powers — France, Britain and the United States. A semi-feudal inheritance was gradually transformed into a constitutional monarchy.

Among notable events during this reign were the opening of Lahainaluna School on Maui in 1831, the oldest high school west of the Rocky Mountains; the establishment on Kauai of the first permanent sugar plantation in 1835; the publication of the first newspaper in the Pacific area (1834); the proclamation of a Constitution (1840); the publication of the first school laws (1841); changes in land ownership concepts through the Great Mahele (1848); and the updating, through a new Constitution, of the structures of government (1852).

In February 1843, Lord George Paulet forced cession of the Hawaiian Kingdom to Great Britain, as the result of a dispute between the two countries, but the action was repudiated by Rear Admiral Richard Thomas in July of that same year, and Hawaii's independence was officially recognised. Honolulu's Thomas Square honors his memory.

HONOLULU BECOMES THE CAPITAL

In 1845 King Kamehameha III and the Legislature moved to Honolulu from the capital at Lahaina, on Maui; on August 31, 1850, he declared Honolulu officially to be the capital of the Kingdom.

During the middle of the 19th century, Hawaii was a centre of whaling activity. An infant sugar industry had found a shortage of plantation labour, and in 1852 Chinese were brought into the kingdom by contract. Thus began the stream of imported labour which lasted until 1946. The first Japanese came in 1868, while Filipinos started arriving at a much later date. Koreans, Portuguese and Puerto Ricans are among the other national groups brought to the islands.

The growing importance of sugar was reflected in Hawaii's political picture during the next few decades. The sugar planters favoured annexation of Hawaii by the United States to establish a firm market for the product. The Hawaiian monarchs, on the other hand, intermittently attempted to establish and implement a policy of Hawaii for the Hawaiians.

During the reigns of Kamehameha's grandson, Alexander Liholiho, who ruled as Kamehameha IV (1855–1863), and his brother,

Lot Kamehameha, Kamehameha V (1863–1872), there was a succession of inconclusive wrangles over the constitution between those insistent on limiting suffrage and strengthening the power of the throne, and those wishing to extend the franchise and limit the powers of the monarch.

With the death of Kamehameha V, the line of direct descendents of Kamehameha ended, and the legislature, following a plebiscite, elected Prince William C. Lunalilo as King. He died a year later, and David Kalakaua was elected his successor. Disorders sparked by adherents of his rival contender, Dowager Queen Emma, widow of Kamehameha IV, broke out in Honolulu when the results became known, and the government was forced to call upon American and British marines to restore order.

Kalakaua brought to fruition negotiations with the United States which were initiated by Lunalilo, and in 1875 a treaty of reciprocity was signed between the two nations. By its terms, Hawaii assured itself of a market for sugar in the United States, and upon its renewal in 1887 the US secured the exclusive use of Pearl Harbour as a coaling station.

Despite his being known as the Merry Monarch, (he wrote the State Song "Hawaii Ponoi") Kalakaua's reign (1874–1891) was a stormy one. He was continually battling for an increase in the personal authority of the King. He dreamed of a Polynesian empire. He made a trip around the world and while in Japan proposed a marriage alliance with the Emperor's family. His efforts, however, were unsuccessful, and under pressure he signed a new constitution in 1887 which further curbed his power, and set up a cabinet-type government responsible to the Legislature. This led, in 1889, to an unsuccessful insurrection by those opposed to the new constitution and its reform measures.

Kalakaua died in 1891 during a visit to San Francisco, and was succeeded by his sister, Liliuokalani. The last Hawaiian monarch, she reigned less than two years. Her policy was to eliminate the restrictions which had been placed on the monarchy, and to this end she attempted to proclaim still another constitution. This led in 1893 to a bloodless 'revolution', her deposition as Queen, and the formation of a provisional government under the leadership of Sanford Ballard Dole.

The Provisional Government requested annexation by the

United States, but President Grover Cleveland was not in sympathy with the Provisional Government or with the revolution, and refused. The Provisional Government then converted Hawaii into a Republic and Dole was proclaimed President in 1894.

ANNEXATION

President William McKinley had a more sympathetic attitude regarding annexation, and the outbreak of the Spanish-American War in 1898 brought matters to a head. Hawaii's strategic military importance in the Pacific was recognised, particularly its potential threat to the United States were another great power to occupy the islands. By Joint Resolution of Congress, the islands were officially annexed, and formal transfer of sovereignty was made on August 12, 1898. The new possession was then organised as a Territory and Dole was appointed its first Governor, taking office on June 14, 1900. The first Territorial Legislature convened on February 20, 1901.

During this period, a young cousin of S.B. Dole who had come to Hawaii from New England to seek his fortune, established a second major industry. James D. Dole, continuing experiments with pineapple which had been made by others, finally found a variety that would grow successfully, and he made his first canned pinneapple pack in 1903, producing 1,893 cases. From this beginning came Hawaii's great pineapple industry of today.

Hawaii's people participated in World War I, but Hawaii was actually a backwash of that great struggle. During the 1920s increased efforts to promote Hawaii for tourists were initiated.

In 1927, army lieutenants Lester Maitland and Alter Hegenberger made the first successful non-stop flight from the Mainland, marking the arrival of the trans-Pacific air age in Hawaii. Commercial inter-island air service began two years later. Radio-telephone service among the islands and to the Mainland was established in 1931, and extended to Europe and South America in 1932. (A telephone system had first been established in Hawaii in 1878.)

The effects of the Great Depression in the 1930s were not as serious in Hawaii as they were in more industrialised areas. With growing international tensions, and particularly the aggressions of Japan in the Far East, the 30s saw a build-up of American military power in Hawaii. They also saw the binding of Hawaii closer to the

Mainland by Pan American World Airways' inauguration of regular commercial passenger flights in 1936.

International tensions burst into flame at 7.55am on the morning of December 7, 1941, when the first Japanese bombs fell on Pearl Harbour, causing nearly 4,000 casualties, and seriously crippling the great American fleet berthed there. Hawaii quickly mushroomed into an armed camp, and was the nerve centre of America's whole Pacific war effort. The joyous celebration of V-J Day on August 14, 1945, was heartfelt.

The Japanese population of Hawaii was the object of some suspicion at the beginning of World War II. This was completely eliminated by the 442nd Regimental Combat Team, composed largely of Nisei (second generation American of Japanese ancestry) from Hawaii, which became the most decorated outfit of the war.

Hawaii spent the greater part of the war under martial law, or a modified concept of it with blackouts, curfews and similar regulations.

A law permitting organisation of agricultural workers, passed by the Territorial Legislature in 1945, brought major labour organisation to the islands within a year.

The late 40s were marred by a series of labour-management conflicts including the very serious waterfront strike of 1949 which lasted six months.

With the outbreak of the Korean conflict in 1950, Hawaii was again called upon. The unpreparedness of the nation as a whole led to a particularly heavy demand on Hawaii, closest to the conflict, and Hawaii's people suffered more military casualties per capita than any other state. Since the end of the Korean conflict, Hawaii has enjoyed economic growth.

STATEHOOD

From the 1930s through the 50s the dominant political theme in Hawaii was Statehood. First proposed during the reign of Kamehameha III, it became a more defined goal shortly after World War I, when Hawaii's Delegate to Congress, Prince Jonah Kuhio Kalanianaole, introduced a bill to that effect. More strenuous efforts were made in the 1930s, when the late Samuel Wilder King was Delegate, and this effort was continued after World War II by Delegate Joseph Rider Farrington, and after his death, by his

widow, Delegate Elizabeth Farrington. A plebiscite showing a
2-to-1 vote in favour of Statehood was conducted in 1940. A
Constitutional Convention which wrote Hawaii's modern constitution was held in 1950.

All these efforts finally culminated in 1959, when John A. Burns
was Delegate, and both Houses of Congress passed the necessary
legislation, the Senate on March 11, and the House on March 12.
Hawaii officially entered the American Union as the 50th State on
Admission Day, August 21, 1959.

William F. Quinn was Hawaii's first elected Governor. The
second was John A. Burns, who served 12 years. He died on April
5, 1975. Third was George R. Ariyoshi, elected to his third and
final term in 1982. John Waihee is 4th.

On April 23, 1959, the last Territorial Legislature officially
designated "The Aloha State" as the official 'popular' name for the
State of Hawaii.

The State's motto is "Ua mau ke ea o ka aina i ka pono" which
means "The life of the land is perpetuated in righteousness". The
saying is attributed to King Kamehameha III as of July 31, 1843,
when the Hawaiian flag once more was raised after a brief period of
unauthorised usurpation of authority by a British admiral.

The State flag has eight stripes (representing the eight major
islands), of white, red and blue. The field closely resembles the
Union Jack of Great Britain, from which the original flag was
designed.

OFFICIAL EMBLEMS

For its official flower the State of Hawaii has chosen the yellow
hibiscus grown throughout the islands. More than five thousand
types of hibiscus hybrids have been identified.

Hawaii's State tree is the indigenous kukui, better known as the
candlenut. The nuts of this tree provided the ancient Hawaiians
with light, oil, relishes, and medicines. By joint resolution, the
Legislature of Hawaii also established official flowers and colours
for each island, as follows:

Hawaii Island	Red Lehua (Ohia)	Red
Maui	Lokelani (Pink Cottage Rose)	Pink
Molokai	White Kukui Blossom	Green
Kahoolawe	Hinahina (Beach Heliotrope)	Grey

Lanai	Kaunaoa (Yellow & Orange Air Plant)	Yellow
Oahu	Ilima	Yellow
Kauai	Mokihana (Green Berry)	Purple
Niihau	White Pupu Shell	White

The Nene (pronounced 'nay-nay'), a variety of goose, is the State bird. The largest land bird, it has adapted itself to live in harsh lava country, by transforming webbed feet to a claw-like shape, and modifying wing structure for shorter flights.

A century ago nene were abundant on the islands of Maui and Hawaii. Hunting wild animals all but destroyed the species until they were protected by law and a restoration project established in 1949. Today there are a few hundred wild nene and they are on the increase. Birds raised in captivity are released to join them.

In 1985 State Legislature designated the small, colourful humu-humunukunuku-a-pua'a, or rectangular triggerfish, as the official fish of the State. The 1979 Legislature designated the humpback whale, an annual visitor to Hawaiian waters, as the State's official marine mammal.

CLIMATE

Hawaii's climate pattern is a combination of cooling trade winds and equable temperatures throughout the year. Rarely are there severe storms of any kind.

The north-easterly trade winds bring the rain-bearing clouds, which are caught by the mountains. Thus, there is an enormous range of rainfall, with the windward sides of the islands being generally wetter than the leeward.

Waialeale on the Island of Kauai has an average annual rainfall of 11,455mm (451 inches), and is one of the two wettest spots on earth although there are areas on the same island, only a few kilometres away, which have a rainfall of less than 508mm (20 inches) a year. The driest spot recorded is Puako, on the Big Island, with an average annual rainfall of 240mm (9.47 inches).

The highest official temperature recorded in downtown Hono-lulu was 31C (88F); the lowest was 13.8C (57F). Snow is found during winter months on the summits of Mauna Kea and Mauna

Loa. The highest temperature ever recorded in the State was 38C (100F), in 1931.

POPULATION

The total population of the island group is approximately 1,082,500, with about half under the age 30. The median age was 31.5 in 1987.

Everyone in Hawaii is a member of an ethnic minority. No single racial group constitutes more than about one-third of the population.

In an American context, the various peoples of Asia have followed a pattern similar to that set by European immigrants to other areas of the United States. The second and third generations have become thoroughly Americanised, and have produced many successful professional and technical people.

LANGUAGE

While ancestral languages are still heard in Hawaii, English is universally used. The native Hawaiian language is also an official State language, and it is often used on emblems and symbols representative of the State. This language is gradually disappearing though, being rarely spoken at home, and taught in only a few schools and at the University of Hawaii.

However, most of the place names and street names are in Hawaiian, so a few words, and a guide to pronunciation, will at least make you sound like a native.

The Hawaiian alphabet consists of seven consonants (h, k, l, m, n, p and w) and the five vowels (a, e, i, o, u). All the vowels in a word are pronounced, and some words contain a glottal stop (') instead of a written consonant.

The consonants are pronounced the same as in English, except that 'w' when it follows 'e' or 'i', is pronounced as a 'v'. The vowels are pronounced as follows:

a as in tar
e as in red
i as in bee
o as in old
u as in rude

'ae	yes
aikane	friend
ala	road, path
alii	chief, royalty
aloha	welcome, greetings, love, farewell
'a'ole	no
haole	Caucasian
hapa	part, half
hele mai	come here
holoku	fitted ankle-length dress with train
holomu'u	fitted ankle-length dress
huhu	angry
hula	Hawaiian dance
iki	small, little
ipo	sweetheart, lover
kahili	feather standard
kahuna	priest, expert
kai	sea
kala	money
kamaaina	native, local resident
kane	male, husband
kapu	forbidden, keep out
keiki	child
kokua	help
lei	garland, wreath
lua	toilet
mahalo	thanks
maika'i	good, fine
malo	loin cloth
manu	bird
manuahi	free, gratis
mauna	mountain
mele	song
moana	ocean
mu'umu'u	loose-fitting dress
nani	beautiful
ne'i	this place
nui	big, large
'ono	tasty, delicious

pa'u	wrap-around skirt
pehea'oe	how are you?
poi	cooked taro corn pounded into paste
pua	flower, blossom
pua'a	pork, pig
pupu	shell
tutu	grandmother
wahine	female, wife
wai	fresh water
wikiwiki	hurry, fast.

RELIGION

Hawaii's religions are as diverse as its cultural heritage. The missionaries who arrived in 1820 were mostly Congregationalists, followed in 1827 by Roman Catholics. In the Constitution of 1840, freedom of worship was guaranteed for all religions.

Later arrivals of thousands of Portuguese and Filipino immigrants greatly increased Catholic numbers in the islands.

The Latter-Day Saints (Mormon) began work in 1850, and the Methodists arrived in 1854. In 1862 Kamehameha IV invited the Anglican Church to establish itself in Hawaii.

Meanwhile, the arrival of the first Chinese contract labourers in 1852 saw the establishment of Chinese temples, some Confucianists, some Taoist, and some Buddhist.

Similarly, Japanese forms of religion followed in 1885. Five of the main forms of Mahayana Buddhism were established in Hawaii: Shingon, Jodo, Jodo Shin (Hongwanji), Zen (Soto) and Nichiren. The Japanese also brought Shinto shrines of many varieties.

Lutherans were established in 1883, Seventh-day Adventists in 1885, the Salvation Army in 1894, Christian Scientists in 1902, Northern Baptists in 1930, Southern Baptists in 1940, Unitarians in 1953, and Presbyterians in 1959. The Religious Society of Friends (Quakers) also have an establishment. The first Jewish synagogue was established in 1950.

Hawaii's many beautiful church buildings include the Mormon Temple at Laie, Our Lady of Peace Cathedral, St Andrew's Cathedral, Central Union Church, The First Church of Christ

Scientist, and Kawaiahao Church on Oahu; Kaahumanu Church, Maui, St Benedict's, Hawaii; and Wailoi Church, Kauai. There are many contemporary-styled churches as well as Buddhist temples and ancient Hawaiian heiaus.

FESTIVALS

In January or early February, Hawaii celebrates the Narcissus Festival, for the Chinese New Year, and selects a Narcissus Queen to reign for the year.

In late March or April comes the Cherry Blossom Festival, with its Cherry Blossom Queen, inspired by the cherry blossom season in Japan. A St Patrick's Day parade is held March 17. Prince Kuhio Day on March 26 is a State holiday.

Also held in the spring is Hilo's Merrie Monarch Festival featuring competitions between Hawaii's best hula halau (schools).

Lei Day is celebrated on May 1, with gorgeous displays of flower leis.

Kamehameha Day on June 11 is a State holiday, with parades and pageants.

Fiesta Filipina is an annual festival sponsored by the United Filipino Council of Hawaii, and is usually held in June.

During July and August the Bon Odori, a Buddhist festival with dances, is staged. Summer also sees a 50th State Fair. Aloha Week Festivals, filled with Hawaiian pageantry and music, come in September. Festivities are held throughout the State featuring dances and craft demonstrations. Admission Day, another State holiday, is the third Friday in August.

Okinawans, Portuguese, Samoans, Koreans and others have festivals and commemorations at various times.

Despite the warmer weather, Christmas is celebrated in Hawaii in the same way as on the Mainland. Large shipments of Christmas trees are brought in from the Pacific Northwest every year.

Such national holidays as President's Day, Memorial Day, Independence Day, Labor Day, Veterans' Day and Thanksgiving are also celebrated. Several of these have been converted into three-day weekend holidays by State law. New Year's Day, and Martin Luther King Day, January 16, are also observed.

ENTRY REGULATIONS

Valid passports are required by all except Canadian nationals with an ID card, and British subjects holding a valid British passport and proof of their status as a 'landed immigrant' in Canada.

Visas are required by all except Canadian and British subject who comply with the passport conditions.

The following goods may be imported without incurring customs duty:

200 cigarettes, or 50 cigars, or 3lb of tobacco, or proportionate amounts of each.

1 litre of alcoholic beverage (age 21 or over).

Gifts or articles up to a value of US$300.

Health Regulations

No vaccination certificates are required, except for yellow fever if arriving from an infected or endemic area.

Currency Restrictions

All import and export currency transactions of over US$5,000 must be reported to US Customs. All gold coins and any quantity of gold must be declared before export. Otherwise there are no restrictions on the import and export of either local or foreign currency.

EMBASSIES

Australia	:	Australian Consulate-General, 1000 Bishop Street, Honolulu, ph 524 5050.
New Zealand	:	No resident representative. Refer to NZ Consulate-General, Tishman Building, 10960 Wilshire Boulevard, Los Angeles, ph (213) 477 8241.
Canada	:	No resident representative. Refer to Consulate-General of Canada, 1 Maritime Plaza, Golden Gateway Centre, San Francisco. ph (415) 981 2670.
U.K.	:	No resident representative. Refer to British Consulate-General, 3701 Wilshire Boulevard, Los Angeles, ph (213) 385 7381.

MONEY

Currency is the United States Dollar (US$) which equals 100 cents. Notes are in denominations of $1, $2, $5, $10, $20, $50 and $100. Coins are in denominations of 1c, 5c (nickel), 10c (dime), 25c (quarter) and 50c.

Approximate exchange rates are:

A$ = US$0.76
NZ$ = US$0.60
Can$ = US$0.80
UK£ = US$1.60

COMMUNICATIONS

With a network composed of undersea cables and satellite communication systems, Hawaii serves as the communications hub of the Pacific. These systems provide two-way voice, data and television services to North America, Australia and Asia, and other Pacific Basin areas. Telephone service through Hawaii is provided by a major company, Hawaiian Telephone Co. The Country Code is 1, and the Area Code is 808.

Hawaii is served by nine daily newspapers, several weekly and semi-weekly papers and numerous magazines, as well as The Associated Press, United Press International and their affiliates. The two major daily newspapers are the afternoon Honolulu Star-Bulletin and the morning Honolulu Advertiser.

There are fourteen commercial and two public television stations, and nine cable television companies. There are also 47 commercial and public radio stations, 20 of them FM.

MISCELLANEOUS

Local time is GMT–10. There is no daylight saving in Hawaii.

Opening Hours
Banks: 8.30am–3pm Mon–Thurs, 8.30am–6pm Fri.
Businesses: 8am–5pm Mon–Fri.
Shops: 9am–9pm Mon–Sat. Some shops open Sunday.

Credit Cards are widely accepted.

There is a departure tax of US$2.00.

Electricity supply is 120 volts AC.

Health

The local tap water is considered safe to drink. Milk is pasteurised and dairy products are safe. Local meat, poultry, seafood, fruit and vegetables are generally considered safe to eat.

Hawaii has high health standards. Life expectancy at birth in 1979–81 was 77.02 years, the highest of any of the 50 states. In 1988 there were 2,150 physicians and surgeons, 847 dentists, 7088 registered nurses, and 469 pharmacists licensed and residing in Hawaii. In 1986 there were 23 acute care hospitals, 36 long term care and 9 specialty care facilities.

Waipio Valley

TRAVEL INFORMATION

HOW TO GET THERE

By Air
The international airport is Honolulu, about 6km (4 miles) north-west of Honolulu, and 10km (6 miles) north-west of Waikiki.

By Sea
The main ports are Honolulu and Lahaina. The following cruise lines run services to Hawaii — Princess, P & O Sitmar, American Hawaii, Royal Viking, Cunard, Nauru Pacific and Union Lloyd.

ACCOMMODATION

Finding accommodation in Hawaii is definitely not a problem. There are modern hotels, from the most luxurious to very modest, on all the islands.

Apartments and condominiums are also there in abundance.

LOCAL TRANSPORT

Air
Aloha, Hawaiian Airlines, Royal Hawaiian Commuter Air and Mid Pacific have frequent inter-island services. Discovery Airways will be operating from December 1989.

Road
All the islands have modern bus services.

Taxi
Taxis are plentiful on all islands, and have meters.

Car Hire
There are international and local agencies providing this service. Foreign licences are accepted by all, and an international licence is not required. Traffic drives on the right. The speed limit is 88km/h (60 mph).

FOOD

The great variety of food reflects the multi-racial atmosphere in Hawaii. Immigrants from different parts of the world have brought with them recipes from their homelands, and added them to the traditional Hawaiian fare. As a result, no matter whether you want to dine on Asian, European or Hawaiian, there will still be a large selection to choose from.

The classic Hawaiian luau features a whole pig, skinned and rubbed with rock salt and soya sauce, placed on chicken wire and filled with hot stones from the imu fire. It is cooked along with sweet potatoes, plantains and sometimes laulaus (butterfish and taro shoots wrapped in banana leaves and steamed). The pig is traditionally eaten with the fingers, accompanied by poi (thick paste made from ground taro — which we are not going to guarantee you'll like, but you should try it), opihi (a black, salty, clam-like mollusc) and lomi lomi salmon (salmon rubbed with an onion and tomato marinade).

Chicken luau is another variety, with the chicken cooked with taro tops and coconut cream. This is served mostly with limu (dried seaweed), chopped roasted kukui nuts and paakai rock salt.

Hawaiian breakfasts are enormous, even by American standards, and the fresh fruit is delicious.

SHOPPING

Hawaii is truly a shopper's paradise. Being the 'crossroads of the Pacific', the islands offer an astonishing variety of shops and goods. Fashions from Europe, apparel from the Far East and of course, the ever-present, ever-colourful Aloha attire of Hawaii itself can be purchased. Shops feature artwork from among some of the most talented artists in the world, and sell fine hand-crafted koa wood figurines carved by local artisans.

If jewellery is on your shopping list, you have come to the right place — from inexpensive rings and brooches featuring parsley dipped in gold and decorated with coral, to jade and precious stones either loose or in unique settings.

And, of course, there is the widest range of swimwear available, for all tastes and sizes.

SPORT AND RECREATION

Water sports lead the list since Hawaii has marvellous swimming beaches. Surfing, so popular these days, was the ancient Hawaiian sport of kings. The annual Duke Kahanamoku and Makaha surfing meets have been world famous.

Reefs and offshore areas present unmatched opportunities for scuba and snorkelling enthusiasts. Other beach sports include outrigger canoe rides and catamaran cruises.

Sailing is also very popular. The biennial Transpacific Yacht Race from California to Honolulu is a yachting classic. There is an annual Molokai-to-Oahu canoe race.

There is good deep-sea fishing in Hawaiian waters. Some of the largest marlin in the world have been hooked in island waters. An International Billfish Tournament is held annually in Kona, and the Hawaii Big Game Fishing Club holds two statewide gamefish tournaments each year. Surfcasting and shore fishing are also popular island pastimes, and there is even freshwater trout fishing on Kauai.

Hiking and hunting trails are found in the islands' green mountains. Cabins are available in some state or national park areas, and most islands offer camping sites. Pack trips can also be arranged.

For the golfer, there are many courses on six islands. Also available are many public tennis courts.

Hawaii offers college baseball; a full season of football culminating in the Hula Bowl, Pro Bowl and Aloha Bowl; college basketball; an annual PGA Golf Tournament; and a polo season. Hawaii boasts of the 50,000-seat Aloha Stadium.

Hawaii is also proud of her tradition of Olympic champions ... Duke Kahanamoku held the Olympic 100m sprint championship for nearly 20 years starting in 1912, and created a tradition of champion island swimmers. Young Keala O'Sullivan won a bronze medal in the 1968 Olympic diving competition. David McFaull and Michael Rothwell won silver medals in the 1976 Olympic Tornado Class boat racing finals.

In December, the annual Honolulu Marathon is held. It is one of the most popular in the US.

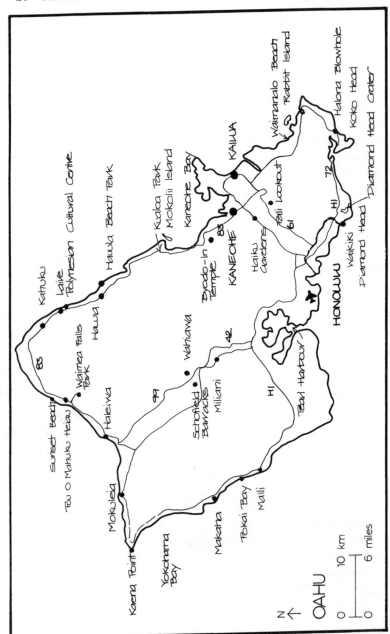

OAHU

Known as "The Gathering Place", Ohau was once the common meeting ground for Hawaii's island kings. It is probably the best known of the Hawaiian Islands, because it is home to Honolulu, Waikiki, Diamond Head and Pearl Harbour.

Oahu is the third largest island in the group, with a population of approximately 900,000. The only royal palace in the United States is found on this island.

It is estimated that around 4,000,000 people a year visit Oahu, mainly staying in the Honolulu-Waikiki area.

Honolulu is a modern city, with tall buildings, broad streets and bright lights. It has been the capital of the State since February 1845, when King Kamehameha III took up residence in the city.

HOW TO GET THERE

Air America has six flights leaving the American Mainland for Honolulu international airport every week.

Hawaiian Airlines fly to Honolulu from:
  Seattle — daily.
  San Francisco — daily.
  Portland — daily.
  Los Angeles — daily.
  Las Vegas — Thursday and Sunday.
  Auckland — Wednesday.
  Sydney — Friday.

Qantas has flights to Honolulu from:
  Sydney — daily except Monday.
  Melbourne — Wednesday, Thursday, Friday and Sunday.
  Auckland — Tuesday, Wednesday, Friday and Sunday.
  Vancouver — Thursday and Saturday.
  San Francisco — Friday and Sunday.

Continental Airlines fly to Honolulu from:
  London — 5 flights per week.

Los Angeles — 5 flights per week.
San Francisco — daily.
Chicago — daily except Sunday.
New York — daily except Sunday.
Sydney — daily.
Melbourne — daily.
Auckland — daily.
Vancouver — Friday, Saturday and Sunday.

Singapore Airlines have flights to Honolulu from:
Los Angeles — Wednesday, Friday and Sunday.
San Francisco — daily.

Air New Zealand flies to Honolulu from:
Los Angeles — Tuesday, Wednesday, Saturday and Sunday.
Vancouver — Sunday.
Auckland — Monday, Tuesday, Wednesday, Thursday and Friday.
Christchurch — Monday, Tuesday, Wednesday, Thursday and Friday.
Brisbane — Tuesday and Wednesday.
Melbourne — Wednesday.
Sydney — Monday, Wednesday and Friday.

TOURIST INFORMATION

Hawaii Visitors' Bureau, Suite 801, Waikiki Business Plaza, 2270 Kalakaua Avenue, Honolulu, ph 923 1811.
'Guide to Oahu' is a free magazine, published every Friday, which has a wealth of information, and special offers and coupons.

ACCOMMODATION

If we were to list all the accommodation available on Oahu, we would have pages and pages of confusing information. We have therefore decided not to include the luxury hotels, which range from US$100 to US$325 per person per night in a standard double room, but instead have listed the rooms available for less than $100 per person per night. The higher price range are fully air-conditioned, but the lower bracket may be partially air-conditioned, or only have fans.

Holiday Inn-Honolulu Airport, 3401 Nimitz Highway, Honolulu, ph 836 0661 — $91–95; Waikiki Beachcomber Hotel, 2300 Kalakaua Avenue, Honolulu, ph 922 4646 — $89–95; Best Western Plaza Hotel-Honolulu International Airport, 3253 N. Nimitz Highway, Honolulu, ph 836 3636 — $89–93; Sheraton Makaha Resort and Country Club, 84–626 Makaha Valley Road, Waianae, ph 695 9511 — leeward Oahu — $85–95; Outrigger Reef Hotel, 2169 Kaila Road, Honolulu, ph 923 3111 — on Waikiki beach — $85–95; Ala Moana Hotel, 410 Atkinson Drive, Honolulu, ph 955 4811 — Waikiki area — $90; Waikiki Parc Hotel, 2233 Helumoa Road, Honolulu, ph 921 7272 — $90; Outrigger Prince Kuhio, 2500 Kuhio Avenue, Honolulu, ph 922 0811 — Waikiki area — $80–90; Kaimana Villa Condominium Hotel, 2550 Kuhio Avenue, Honolulu, ph 923 4511 — Waikiki area — $65–90.

Park Shore Hotel, 2586 Kalakaua Avenue, Honolulu, ph 923 0411 — Waikiki area — $80–85; Pacific Monarch Condominium Apartments, 142 Uluniu Avenue, Honolulu, ph 923 9805 — Waikiki area — $75–85; Princess Kaiulani Hotel, 120 Kaiulani Avenue, Honolulu, ph 922 5811 — Waikiki area — $75–85; Queen Kapiolani Hotel, 150 Kapahulu Avenue, Honolulu, ph 922 1941 — Waikiki area — $72–85; Waikiki Plaza Hotel, 245 Kalakaua Avenue, Honolulu, ph 955 6363 — Waikiki area — $60–85; Waikiki Gateway Hotel, 2070 Kalakaua Avenue, Honolulu, ph 955 3741 — $49–85; Coral Reef Hotel, 2299 Kuhio Avenue, Honolulu, ph 922 1262 — Waikiki area — $53–84; Ewa Hotel Waikiki, 2555 Cartwright Road, Honolulu, ph 922 1677 — $70–80; Best Western Waikiki Plaza Hotel, 2045 Kalakaua Avenue, Honolulu, ph 955 6363 — $68–80; Waikiki Parkside Hotel, 1850 Ala Moana Boulevard, Honolulu, ph 955 1567 — $80.

Miramar At Waikiki Hotel, 2345 Kuhio Avenue, Honolulu, ph 922 2077 — $68–78; Aston Waikiki Beach Tower, 2470 Kalakaua Avenue, Honolulu, ph 926 6400 — condominiums across from Waikiki Beach — $49–76; Aston Honolulu Prince Hotel, 415 Nahua Street, Honolulu, ph 922 1616 — Waikiki area — $49–76; Hawaiiana Hotel, 260 Beach Walk, Honolulu, ph 923 3811 — Waikiki area — $70–75; Aloha Surf Hotel, 444 Kanekapolei Street, Honolulu, ph 923 0222 — Waikiki area — $65–75;

Outrigger West Hotel, 2330 Kuhia Avenue, Honolulu, ph 922 5022 — Waikiki area — $65–75; Royal Kuhio, 2240 Kuhio Avenue, Honolulu, ph 923 2502 — condominium apartments in Waikiki area — $70; Waikiki Royal, 255 Beach Walk, Honolulu —apartment hotel in Waikiki area — $70; Outrigger East Hotel, 150 Kalulani Avenue, Honolulu, ph 922 5353 — Waikiki area — $60–70; Maile Court, 2058 Kuhio Avenue, Honolulu, ph 947 2828 —hotel-condominium in Waikiki area — $55–70; Outrigger Village Hotel, 240 Lewers Street, Honolulu, ph 923 3881 — Waikiki area — $60–70; Outrigger Reef Towers, 227 Lewers Street, Honolulu, ph 924 8844 — Waikiki area — $60–70.

White Sands Waikiki Resort Hotel, 431 Nohonani Street, Honolulu, ph 923 7336 — $52–69; Waikiki Resort Hotel, 2460 Koa Avenue, Honolulu, ph 922 4911 — Waikiki area — $64–68; Outrigger Reef Lanais Hotel, 225 Saratoga Road, Honolulu, ph 923 3881 — $60–65; Waikiki Grand, 134 Kapahulu Avenue, Honolulu, ph 923 1511 — apartment hotel — $55–65; Pagoda Hotel, 1525 Rycroft Street, Honolulu, ph 941 6611 — Ala Moana area — $54–65; Hawaiian Monarch Hotel, 444 Niu Street, Honolulu, ph 949 3911 — Waikiki area — $49–65.

Quality Inn Waikiki-Diamond Head Hotel, 175 Paoakalani Avenue, Honolulu, ph 922 4671 — $59; Outrigger Coral Seas Hotel, 250 Lewers Street, Honolulu, ph 923 3881 — Waikiki area — $45–56; Waikiki Marina Hotel, 1956 Ala Moana Boulevard, Honolulu, ph 955 0714 — $45–50; Royal Grove, 151 Uluniu Avenue, Honolulu, ph 923 7691 — apartment hotel — $30–50.

Waikiki Sand Villa Hotel, 2375 Ala Wai Boulevard, Honolulu, ph 922 4744 — $39–49; Waikiki Circle Hotel, 2464 Kalakaua Avenue, Honolulu, ph 923 1571 — $38–47; Outrigger Waikiki Surf Hotel, 2200 Kuhio Avenue, Honolulu, ph 923 7671 — $40–45; Malihini Hotel, 217 Saratoga Road, Honolulu, ph 923 9644 — hotel and apartments in Waikiki area — $35–40; Waikiki Prince Hotel, 2431 Prince Edward Street, Honolulu, ph 922 1544 — Waikiki area — $27–32.

PACKAGE TOURS

Package tours are an economical way of visiting Hawaii, and take the worry out of such things as airport transfers. All the airlines which fly to the islands have tours on offer which include return air fares and accommodation, often in the luxury hotels.

For example, Hawaiian Airlines' package tours include — return airfares Sydney-Honolulu, 6 nights at New Otani Hotel, with free inter-island return flights to an Hawaiian Island of your choice for A$1,167 twin share. The same deal, but staying at the Waikiki Parc Hotel, for A$1,198, or at the Ilukai for A$1,206, or at the Hawaiian Regent for A$1,318.

Hawaiian Airlines can also arrange the accommodation on the outer islands at a very competitive price, and offer their 'Islands in the Sky' tour, a day/air/ground tour of the 8 islands for US$177.32.

Hawaii is also a good place to break the long flight from the US to Australia/New Zealand, or vice versa, and three to five day stopovers can be arranged by whichever airline you are using, including inexpensive accommodation and transfers between the airport and your hotel. You should check with your local travel agent for information on current packages available.

Generally Qantas Jetabout has Mini Stay packages offering 2 nights accommodation, including taxes, at the Sheraton Waikiki and return airport transfers by taxi for A$176, with an extra night for A$72. For Mini Stay packages out of the Waikiki area, an example is two nights accommodation, including taxes, at the Sheraton Makaha Resort and Country Club, plus 2 days car hire for A$154 twin share, with an extra night for A$77.

LOCAL TRANSPORT

The Honolulu International Airport is located 13km (8 miles) from Waikiki, about 30 minutes by taxi. If you are an independent traveller, taxi is one way to get to your hotel, but it's expensive, the ride to Waikiki averaging about US$13 to US$15, with a 25c charge per suitcase. For pick-up ring 836 0011.

Other choices are:

Airport Motorcoach
This mini-bus service costs US$3.50 per adult and US$2 per child, which includes two suitcases and a carry-on. For rides from the Airport to Waikiki there has to be at least 12 people, and reservations have to be made at least a couple of days in advance.

From Waikiki to the Airport, ph 926 4747 at least two to three days ahead of flight time, or at least four hours in advance to book a seat. The first run from Waikiki is at 6.30am, arriving at 7.30am, then every 51 minutes until 9.15pm. They will pick-up at nearly all major hotels, as well as their regular stops at the Waikiki Plaza, the Princess Kaiulani, and the Ala Moana hotels.

Waikiki Express
Waikiki Express charges US$4.75 per person from the Airport to Waikiki, and reservations are requested. The reservations line is open from 5am–11pm daily, ph 942 2177. The mini-vans run 5am–midnight daily.

Reservations are also required for the service to the Airport from Waikiki, at least a day before departure, for international flights, and at least an hour and a half before an inter-island flight. The vans run every half hour and pick up at any Waikiki hotel up to Diamond Head. The fare is also US$4.75.

Gray Line
The most obvious buses at the airport, because of their large 'Airporter' signs, and their 40 ft length, Gray Line buses run from the Airport to Waikiki every 20 minutes from the main terminal. The service to the Airport is every hour, and the cost is US$5 per person one way, either way.

Gray Line also operates a fleet of limos, and the charges are US$7.75 from the Airport to Waikiki, and US$7.28 from Waikiki to the Airport, per person.

City Buses
TheBus (no we haven't left out the space, that it what it is called) is an extremely good bus service, but not really practicable for airport transfers, as there is no luggage space. What you can't fit on your lap you have to make other arrangements to transport.

But for sightseeing, or simply getting around the Island, you can't beat TheBus. The fare is 60c per adult, 25c per youth, and no charge for children 5 or under when accompanied by an adult, from anywhere to anywhere, as long as you keep going in the same direction. Request a free transfer for each fare paid if more than one bus is to be used during one continuous trip.

The buses display route numbers and destinations above the driver. You enter through the front door and deposit the exact fare, in coins, in the box. The driver does not carry change. When you wish to alight, signal the driver to stop by pulling the cord along the windows, or by pushing the yellow stip. Exit is through the centre door after the green light appears.

'Honolulu & Oahu by TheBus' is an inexpensive sightseeing map/guide which you will find invaluable. For Bus Information ph 531 1611, 5.30am–10pm.

Car Rental

If you are travelling in the peak holiday seasons (August, Christmas/New Year, February) it is wise to pre-book a hire car, because although there are plenty to choose from, there are plenty of visitors as well. Your hotel desk will probably be able to arrange a car for you or following are some names and address in Honolulu:

Aloha Funway Rentals, 2976 Koapaka Street, ph 834 1016, 1984 Kalakaua Avenue, ph 942 9696; 2025 Kalakaua Avenue, ph 946 2766; 1944 Kalakaua Avenue, ph 947 4579; 1778 Ala Moana Boulevard, ph 945 3677.

Avis Rent-A-Car, 417 Lele Street, ph 834 5524; 148 Kaiulani Avenue, ph 924 1688; Honolulu International Airport, ph 834 5536.

Budget Rent-A-Car, P.O. Box 15188, ph 922 7221, 922 3600.

Cruisin' Classics, 2139 Kuhio Avenue, ph 531 1954.

Dollar Rent-A-Car, 1600 Kapiolani Boulevard, Suite 825, ph 926 4200.

GECC Hawaii-Leasing Co, 1210 N. Nimitz Highway, ph 545 4060.

Hertz Rent-A-Car, 233 Keawe Street, Suite 625, ph 523 5181; 2424 Kalakaua Avenue, ph 922 5344; Honolulu International Airport, ph 835 2511.

National Car Rental, 3223 N. Nimitz Highway, ph 836 2655; 1778 Ala Moana Boulevard, ph 922 3331.

Roberts Hawaii, 444 Hobron Lane, 5th Floor, ph 947 393.

Tropical Rent-A-Car, 550 Paiea Street, Suite 203, ph 836 0788; Pacific Beach Hotel, 2490 Kalakaua Avenue, ph 922 2385; 2002 Kalakaua Avenue, ph 949 2002.

United Car Rental Systems, 234 Beach Walk, ph 922 4605; 2352 Kalakaua Avenue, ph 923 0052.

Distance and Driving Time
From Waikiki to:
Downtown Honolulu — 6km (4 miles), 15 minutes.
Pali Lookout — 14km (9 miles), 20 minutes.
Laie (via Pali) — 61km (38 miles), 1 hour 15 minutes.
Pearl Harbour — 18km (11 miles), 25 minutes.
Makaha — 58km (36 miles), 1 hour.
Hanauma Bay (via Kalanianaole Highway) — 13km (8 miles), 20 minutes.
Makapuu Point — 19km (12 miles), 30 minutes.
Kailua Junction (via Kalanianaole Highway) — 34km (21 miles), 50 minutes.
Circle Trip from Waikiki around Koko Head and return by Pali — 56km (35 miles), 1 hour 15 minutes.
Circle Trip from Waikiki via Pali and return by Laie and Wahiawa — 135km (84 miles), 3 hours 30 minutes.

EATING OUT

There are over 1,000 restaurants on Oahu, so we can't possibly name them all, but we will give you some names and addresses you might like to try. We have rated them by the price of a main course: expensive — $18 and over, moderate — $13–$17, inexpensive — $8–$12, economical — $7 and under.

American
Black Orchid, Restaurant Row, ph 521 3111 — fish, pasta and grills — dancing and entertainment nightly — expensive.

Bobby McGee's Conglomeration, Colony East Hotel, 2885 Kalakaua Avenue, ph 922 1282 — steaks and seafood — dancing — moderate.

Captain's Table, Holiday Inn, 2570 Kalakaua Avenue, ph 922 2511 — seafood, steaks and pasta — expensive.

Kentucky Fried Chicken, 2122–2128 Kalakaua Avenue, ph 923 8211 — budget.

Marco Polo, Waikiki Shopping Plaza (4th floor), ph 922 7733 — steaks, seafood and entertainment — moderate.

Perry's Smorgy Restaurants, Outrigger Waikiki Hotel, ph 926 9872; 2380 Kuhio Avenue, Kanekapolei, ph 926 0184; Coral Seas Hotel, ph 923 3881 — buffets and salads — economical.

The Pottery, 3574 Waialae Avenue, ph 735 5594 — steaks and seafood — economical.

Shasteen's, Hilton Hawaiian Village, 2005 Kalia Road, ph 949 6468 — steaks and seafood — moderate.

Super Chef Gourmet Cuisine, Waikiki Hana Hotel, 2424 Koa Avenue, ph 926 7199 — steaks, seafood and special breakfasts — moderate.

Windows of Hawaii Revolving Restaurant, Ala Moana Building, ph 941 9138 — steaks and seafood — moderate.

Cajun and Creole

New Orleans Bistro, 2139 Kuhio Avenue, ph 926 4444 — breakfast, lunch and dinner plus Sunday brunch — moderate.

German

Hofbrau Waikiki -- International Market Place, 2330 Kalakaua Avenue, ph 923 8982 — moderate.

Greek

It's Greek To Me, Royal Hawaiian Shopping Centre, ph 922 2733 — floorshow — moderate.

Italian

Caffe Guccinni, 2139 Kuhio Avenue (Behind ABC store), ph 922 5287 — economical.

Matteo's, Marine Surf Hotel, 364 Seaside, ph 922 5551 — expensive.

The Noodle Shop, Waikiki Sand Villa Hotel, ph 922 4744 — economical.

Trattoria, Edgewater Hotel, Lewers & Kalia Roads, ph 923 8415 — moderate.

Luaus

Ali'i Luau, Polynesian Cultural Centre, ph 293 3333 — expensive
Germaine's Luau — private beach, pick-ups at major hotels — expensive.

Paradise Cove Luau, West Beach, ph 973-LUAU — expensive.
The Luau, Outrigger Waikiki Hotel, ph 395 0677 — moderate.

Oriental

Bangkok Orchid Cuisine, 131 Kaiulani Avenue (King's Village, 3rd floor), ph 924 7688 — economical.

Benihana of Tokyo, 2005 Kalia Road (Hilton Hawaiian Village), ph 955 5955 — moderate.

Great Wok of China, Royal Hawaiian Shopping Centre, ph 922 5373 — moderate.

Kea's Thai Cuisine, 625 Kapahulu Avenue, ph 737 8240; 1200 Ala Moana Boulevard, ph 533 0533; 1486 S. King Street, ph 947 9988 — moderate.

Kobe Japanese Steak House, 1841 Ala Moana Boulevard, ph 941 4444 — moderate.

Maiko, Ilikai Hotel, 1777 Ala Moana Boulevard, ph 946 5151 — moderate.

Man Lee's Chinese Restaurant, 124 Kapahulu Avenue, ph 922 6005 — economical.

Mekong 11, 1726 S. King Street, ph 941 6184 — moderate.

Odoriko, King's Village, 2400 Koa Avenue, ph 923 7368 — moderate.

Siam Inn, 407 Seaside Avenue, ph 926 8802 — moderate.

Singha Thai Cuisine, 1910 Ala Moana Boulevard, ph 941 2898 — moderate.

Tanaka of Tokyo, Waikiki Shopping Plaza, 2250 Kalakaua Avenue, ph 922 4702 — moderate.

Wo Fat Restaurant (Hawaii's oldest restaurant), 115 North Hotel Street, ph 537 6260 — economical.

Won Kee Seafood Restaurant, Aloha Surf Hotel, 444 Kanekapolei Street, ph 926 7606 — moderate.

Pizza
Pizzeria Uno, 2256 Kuhio Avenue, ph 926 0646 — economical.

Polynesian
Tahitian Lanai, Oceanside of Waikikian Hotel, ph 946 6541 — moderate.

ENTERTAINMENT

There is plenty to do in Downtown Honolulu when the sun goes down. First let's start with good places to spend the Happy Hours:

The Great Wok of China, Royal Hawaiian Shopping Centre, 3rd floor, Building B. Already listed in our restaurant guide, we suggest you arrive early, or just pop in, for the $1 Happy Hour and entertainment from 4–6.30pm, ph 922 5373.

New Orleans Bistro, 2139 Kuhio Avenue, has its Happy, or Cocktail, Hour with pupus and special drink prices from 4–5pm daily, ph 926 4444.

The Noodle Shop, Waikiki Sand Villa Hotel, Kanekapolei at Ala Wai Boulevard — Happy Hour 4–6pm daily with drinks from $1.50, ph 922 4744.

Pizzeria Uno, 2256 Kuhio Avenue, has a very long Happy Hour — from 11am–6pm daily. Prices range from 95c for draft beer to $1.95 for exotic drinks. From 9pm–midnight, Wednesday to Saturday, they have music with Rusty Wilson, ph 926 0646.

Proud Peacock Restaurant, Waimea Falls Park, on the North Shore, ph 638 8531. Happy Hour, with aloha attire, is from 3–7pm.

Studebaker's in Restaurant Row, ph 531 8444, has a $1 cover charge and features 50s and 60s music and entertainment by dancing DJs and waitresses.

Lounges

Benihana in the Hilton Hawaiian Village, 2005 Kalia Road, ph 955 5955. Live music and entertainment in the Piano Bar nightly, except Monday, 7–10pm. No cover charge and no minimum.

Caffe Guccinni, 2139 Kuhio Avenue, ph 922 5287, has a full liquor and wine bar. Open Mon–Sat, 3–11pm and Sun 4–11pm.

Captain's Table Lounge, 2570 Kalakaua Avenue, ph 922 2511, presents Geri Arias and the Paradise Serenaders performing Hawaiian music mixed with country, swing and contemporary music — Fri and Sat, 9.30pm–1.30am.

The Greak Wok of China, Royal Hawaiian Shopping Centre, 3rd floor, ph 922 5373, have old and contemporary Hawaiian music and old-time favourites in the Hideaway Lounge.

New Orleans Bistro, 2139 Kuhio Avenue, ph 926 4444, have live jazz nightly.

The Row is a popular outdoor bar in Restaurant Rowe, ph 528 2345. Open everyday 11am–1.30am with evening entertainment Tues–Fri.

Revues

Sea Life Park, oceanside at Makapuu Point, has night-time shows every Thurs, Fri and Sun, ph 923 1531 or 259 7933.

Society of Seven at the Main Showroom of the Outrigger, 2335 Kalakaua Avenue, ph 922 6408 or 923 0711. One of the best-known happenings in Honolulu, showtimes are 8.30pm and 10.30pm nightly, except Sun, with Wed 8.30pm only.

SHOPPING

There are four large shopping complexes in Honolulu — Ala Moana Shopping Center, one of the world's largest outdoor shopping malls; Ware Warehouse, reminiscent of the seafaring days of Old Hawaii; Pearlridge Shopping Center, with its monorail between buildings; and the Royal Hawaiian Shopping Center. Add to that the hundreds of smaller complexes and individual shops, and you have a shopper's paradise.

A must is the Aloha Flea Market at Aloha Stadium. Eastmark Enterprises arrange a visit on Wed, Sat and Sun from 7.30am–3pm for $6 round trip on the Aloha Flea Market Shuttle and admission inside. This is Hawaii's largest shopping event with more than 1,500 stalls covering 3.5 miles. The coaches have large baggage compartments to take your purchases. Ph 955 4050 (24 hours) for boarding schedules and other information.

Clothing
Benihana Boutique, Hilton Hawaiian Village, ph 955 5955, have racing jackets, tote bags, caps, T-shirts, sweaters and other gift items.

Harley Davidson T-Shirts are available at Skin Deep Tattooing, 2128 Kalakaua Avenue, just behind Zorro's Pizza, ph 924 7460 — open 11am–midnight.

Hilo Hattie, 700 Nimitz Highway, advertise they are open 8.30am–5pm, 365 days a year. You can watch skilled workers turn tropical print fabrics into quality aloha wear for the entire family. They also sell souvenirs, Hawaii videos and books, floral perfumes, tropical jams and candies, jewellery, purses and hats. There is a free Hilo Hattie Bus to and from Waikiki. Ph 537 2926 for information.

Swimsuit Warehouse has four locations — Royal Hawaiian Shopping Centre, 3rd floor, ph 922 8100; Kuhio Mall, ground floor, ph 926 6377; Waikiki Shopping Plaza, 3rd floor, ph 922

5282; 870 Kapahulu Avenue, ph 735 0040. They have over 25,000 designer swimsuits available at extremely competitive prices.

Ujena of California, in The Pavilion at Ward Centre across from Keo's, 1200 Ala Moana Boulevard, stock high-quality, original swimwear, casual wear, exercise wear and leathers, ph 531 0566.

Leather Goods

Glatt Importer, Waikiki Shopping Plaza, 2250 Kalakaua Avenue, Room 522, has a wide range of eelskin items, including purses, wallets, shoes, leather jackets and skirts. Wholesale prices with out-of-state shipping. Open Mon–Sat, 9am–6pm, ph 923 1796.

Leather of The Sea, 2275 Kalakaua Avenue, Suite 1007, ph 923 7615, are the 'World's Largest Wholesaler of Eel Skin Products'. Their showroom has golfbags, wallets, shoes, purses, briefcases, portfolios and other eel, snake and lizard skin products. Open Mon–Sat.

Souvenirs

Dole Pineapple Pavilion on Highway 99 toward the North Shore, ph 531 8855 for bus information. Open daily 9am–5.30pm. Here there is a variety of souvenirs, gifts and islands products at this unique shopping structure. Fresh fruit may be ordered for shipment.

Exotics Hawaii on the ground floor behind the waterfall in the Royal Hawaiian Shopping Center, ph 922 2205, have blooming orchids, boxed for hand-carry and agriculturally inspected, for you to take home. They also have two-inch starter posts of anthuriums, bird of paradise, plumeria, hibiscus and ginger. Please remember that some countries will not let you import plants from overseas.

Wyland Gallery, 66–150 Kamehameha Highway, Haleiwa on the North Shore, has a treasury of many fine works by the popular American environmental artist, creator of Waikiki's 'Whaling Wall'. Works of other artists are also featured. Open daily, 9am–7pm, ph 637 7498.

Chinatown

Unlike the Chinatowns in other American cities, this section of downtown Honolulu is a blend of shops, restaurants and markets displaying not only Chinese goods, but wares and foods typical of the countries of origin of Hawaii's early-day immigrants.

Bounded by Ala Moana Boulevard/N. Nimitz Highway, Nuuanu Avenue, Vineyard Boulevard and the Kapalama Canal, Chinatown's 15-block area is packed with places of interest. It is 10 minutes from Waikiki by City Bus No. 2, or take the Waikiki Trolley to Stop No. 14. If you drive yourself, there is plenty of parking. Oahu Market, off N. King Street, was founded in 1904, and has displays of exotic fruit and vegetables, as well as mouth-watering char siu (roasted pork), opa-kapaka (snapper) and kim chee (pickled cabbage).

Shung Chong Yuein, in Maunakea Street, is a Chinese bakery offering special Chinese treats.

Wo Fat Restaurant, Hotel and Maunakea Streets, is hard to miss because of its pink exterior. The first restaurant on this site was destroyed in the Chinatown fire of 1886. Wat Ging, the proprietor, rebuilt it in time for the fire of 1900. But he persisted, built again, and it has become one of Hawaii's most famous restaurants.

Lai Fong, Nuuanu Avenue, is an antique shop which also specialises in tailor-made clothing. Here you can order a silk brocade cheong sam for as little as $25.

Chinatown Cultural Plaza is a complex housing several exotic cafes, import shops, and an entertainment stage.

SIGHTSEEING

DOWNTOWN HONOLULU

Unlike any other city in the United States, Honolulu has a history of kings, queens and a palace, with all the associated intrigue.

The attractions in this area of Honolulu can be easily explored on foot.

Iolani Palace

Completed in 1882, the building is the only royal palace on American soil, and is where the last two monarchs lived and ruled. It has been entirely renovated, displaying a magnificent interior. Palace tours are conducted Wed–Sat, 9am–2.15pm, and for reservations, ph 522 0832.

Iolani Barracks

Originally situated on Hotel Street, the barracks were moved brick by brick in 1965 to its present position in the palace grounds. It was here that the Royal Guards had its headquarters and home from 1871 to 1893.

Coronation Pavilion
The Royal Hawaiian Band plays each Friday at noon in this small round bandstand. It was originally built in 1883.

King Kamehameha Statue
Located on the ocean side of the Palace, the statue of Hawaii's most loved king, who unified the Hawaiian kingdom, shows him holding a barbed spear in his left hand as a symbol of peace. His right arm is outstretched in a gesture of aloha.

Kawaiahao Church
Dedicated in 1842, the 'Westminster Abbey' of Hawaii offers Sunday services in Hawaiian and English. The church is on S. King Street.

Mission Houses Museum
The oldest existing buildings erected by the first missionary contingent to Honolulu are in the civic centre area.

State Capital
Located directly behind the Iolani Palace, this $24.5m building is the centre of Hawaii's political power. The architectural design shows the state's volcanic and oceanic origins.

Washington Place
The residence of Queen Liliuokalani until her death in 1917, the building is now the home of Hawaii's governors. It is the oldest continuously occupied house on Oahu, having been built in 1846.

St Andrew's Cathedral
Situated on Queen Emma Street, the Cathedral is an English Norman styled church which was built in 1867 largely due to the conversion and support of Queen Emma and King Kamehameha IV.

Aloha Tower
Built in 1926, this 10-storey tower was once Hawaii's tallest building. It is still the official maritime signal point and the state's harbour headquarters. The tower is open to visitors and offers an excellent view of the harbour area.

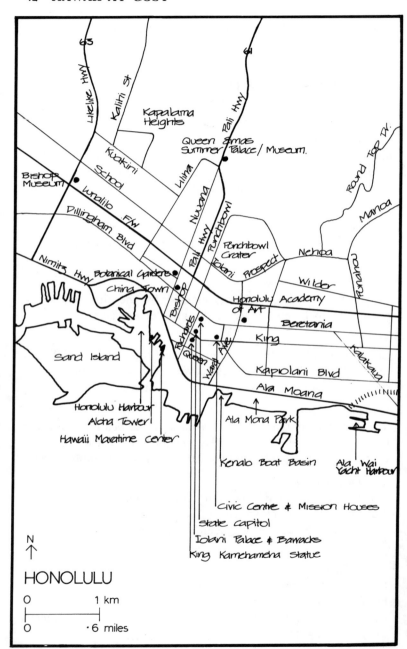

HONOLULU

0   1 km

0   ·6 miles

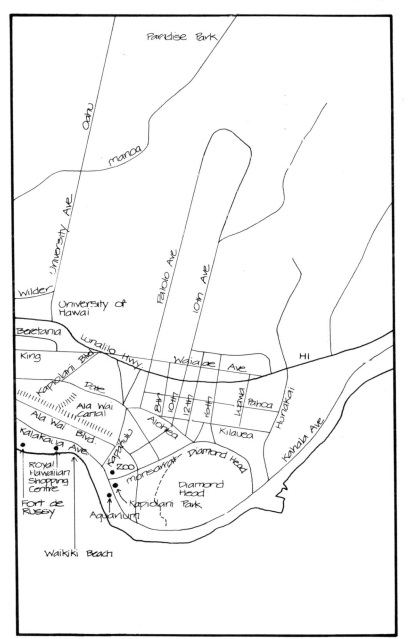

Hawaii Maritime Center
Situated at Honolulu's Pier 7, the complex includes the 6m
Kalakaua Boathouse, a two-storey exhibition of shipping, fishing,
surfing, whales, and other marine objects. The center also has two
museum ships: the *Hokule'a*, a performance-accurate Polynesian
voyaging canoe that serves as the flagship for a canoe display; and
the *Falls of Clyde*, one of the world's last four-masted, full-rigged
sailing vessel. Open daily 9am–5pm. There is an admission fee,
ph 536 6373.

Foster Botanic Garden
On the corner of Vineyard Boulevard and Nuuanu Avenue, in a
8ha (20 acres) setting, the garden features an orchid section,
prehistoric plant area and a special collection of palms.

MIDTOWN HONOLULU
Midtown is bounded by the ocean, Ward Avenue, Beretania
Avenue and Kalakaua Avenue and the Ala Wai Canal. It is the
centre of communications and shopping.
    In this area are the Ala Moana Shopping Center and the Ward
Warehouse Shopping Center, and TheBus terminal at Ala Moana
is the busiest on Oahu.

Ala Moana Park
Ala Moana is the most popular city beach of Honolulu because of
its safe swimming areas, but the sand is very coarse. It is a man-
made beach. In the total area of (76 acres) there are jogging paths,
picnic tables, tennis courts, a bowling green and softball fields.
Nearby are the Aina Moana Park, also known as Magic Island, and
the Ala Wai Yacht Harbour.

Honolulu Academy of Arts
Built in 1927 and accredited by the American Association of
Museums, the Academy is internationally renown for its extensive
collection of Asian and Western Art, and the beauty of its grounds
and buildings. It is a registered national and state historic place.
Located at 900 South Beretania Street, the Academy is open
Tues–Sat, 10am–4pm and Sun 1–5pm. There are free tours Tues,
Wed, Fri and Sat at 11am, Thurs 2pm and Sun 1pm, and there is
no entrance fee. For information ph 538 1006/3693.

Kewalo Boat Basin
It is from here that the tour boats set off for cruises to Diamond Head and Pearl Harbour. Nearby are the John Dominis and Fisherman's Wharf restaurants.

WAIKIKI
Although we think of Waikiki Beach, it is actually a series of beaches, stretching from Duke Kahanamoku Beach in the west to Sans Souci Beach at the Diamond Head end of Kalakaua Avenue. Swimming is good for almost the entire length of the beach, except near the Kapahulu Wall. Keep in mind, though, that these are not the great surfing beaches of Hawaii, there were no waves when I was there.

Waikiki Aquarium
At 2777 Kalakaua Avenue across from Kapiolani Park. A top attraction for visitors, the Aquarium contains a world-famous collection of tropical fish. Open daily 9am–5pm, there is no set admission fee, but a donation of $2.50 is invited from adults, ph 923 9741.

Kapiolani Park
The 88ha (220 acres) park separates Waikiki from the residential area on the south-west of Diamond Head. The Kodak Hula Show, which has been entertaining visitors since 1937, is presented here Tues–Thurs at 10am. There is no admission fee.

Honolulu Zoo
The zoo is at 151 Kapahulu Avenue and is open daily 8.30am–4pm. There is an entry fee. Along with the usual lions, elephants, etc. there are some rare creatures, native to Hawaii, whose ancestors greeted the first settlers.

Fort DeRussy Army Museum
The US Army Museum at Fort DeRussy has ancient Hawaiian weapons as well as weapons and uniforms used by the US forces in campaigns from the Spanish-American War to the Korean War. There are also enlargements of the Honolulu newspapers from the early days of the US involvement in World War II after the invasion of Pearl Harbour. The museum is open Tues–Sun,

10am–4.30pm, and there is no entry fee. Tours by appointment, ph 438 2819/2821.

In the Regional Visitor Center, Fort DeRussy, there is a free exhibition/media show of Pacific life — Tues–Sun, 10am–4.30pm, ph 438 2815.

Diamond Head

Christened by British sailors who mistook the calcite crystals they discovered for diamonds, Diamond Head is one of the most recognisable characteristics of Hawaii. The Hawaiian name for this ancient volcano was Leahi, 'brow of an ahi' probably because its silhouette resembles the profile of the ahi (tuna). Whichever you like to call it, in the sunlight it does seem to sparkle with diamonds.

Diamond Head is a National Natural Landmark and a state monument. Within its crater is a park and a one-mile hiking trail, which leads to a spectacular 232m (760 ft) summit view of Honolulu and the ocean. From Waikiki take the Beach bus east to the corner of Kahala Avenue and Diamond Head Road, and follow the sign posts.

Since 1982, the Clean Air Team has conducted excursions to the summit of Diamond Head. You can meet the team's volunteer leaders at the Honolulu Zoo every Saturday and Sunday at 9am. A small flashlight is recommended for the tunnel along the ascent. Adults are asked to make a $3 donation.

GREATER HONOLULU AND PEARL HARBOUR

Pearl Harbour

Pearl Harbour and the USS Arizona Memorial are among the most visited attractions in Hawaii. The local Department of Business and Economic Development states that over 1.8m people visit this historic site yearly.

Even if you are not old enough to remember the horrific attack on Pearl Harbour by the Japanese on December 7, 1941, bringing the United States into World War II, you will still be impressed with the Arizona Memorial, which is built over the ship's hull. To stand on the memorial, watching the fish swim around the rusting hull and knowing that the bodies of many sailors were never recovered, despite several attempts, cannot fail to move even the most 'been there, done that' type of visitor.

The Arizona Memorial Shuttle takes visitors from Waikiki to the Arizona Memorial Visitor Centre, and aboard the Memorial for $2 each way per person. For information and reservations, ph 926 4747.

If you have your own transport, drive to Pearl Harbour and from the Visitors' Center take the Navy launch to the memorial's dock.

There are also many cruises available to Pearl Harbour and the Arizona, but these, while extremely comfortable and offering cocktails and snacks on board, do not allow you to board the Memorial, they sail around it.

Tied up next to the Memorial ground facility, and open for inspection, is the preserved *USS Bowfin*, the WWII submarine credited with sinking 44 enemy ships. The Pearl Harbour Submarine Base is open for visitors Wed–Sun, 9.30am–5pm.

For information on *USS Bowfin* and the Submarine Base Museum, ph 423 1341. There is an entry fee for both.

Castle Park
Hawaii's first theme park, this family entertainment centre covers over 6ha (14 acres) adjacent to Aloha Stadium, with attractions such as water flumes, bumper boats, miniature race cars and golf courses.

Bishop Museum and Planetarium
At 1525 Bernice Street, the museum houses the world's foremost collection of Hawaiiana and Polynesian antiquities. Open Mon–Sat 9am–5pm, and the first Sun of the month. Entry fee $4.95 adults, $2.50 children 6–17, ph 847 3511.

Queen Emma's Summer Palace
Situated at 2913 Pali Highway in the Nuuana Valley, the palace was built for Queen Emma, wife of Kamehameha IV, as a cool retreat in the late 1800s. Now it is a museum displaying period artifacts. For information ph 595 3167.

Nuuanu Pali Lookout
The Lookout is the site of King Kamehameha's rout of his enemies in the battle that established him as ruler of all the islands. From Waikiki take the H-1 West Freeway, then take the Pali Highway turn off (Exit 21B). A few kilometres further on, turn right just before the Pali tunnel.

The Punchbowl (The National Memorial Cemetery of the Pacific)
Located at 2177 Puowaina Drive, known to the ancient Hawaiians as Puowaina (Hill of Sacrifice), the cemetery is located in the Punchbowl Crater. Over 26,000 American servicemen and women from four wars are buried here, and the names of 26,280 others missing in action are listed on marble walls called the Court of the Missing. There are special ceremonies held here on Memorial Day and Veterans' Day, and a dawn service is held on Easter Sunday.

There is a very good view from The Punchbowl of Pearl Harbour, Honolulu and Waikiki. The cemetery is open daily 8am–6.30pm. For information ph 546 3190.

Manoa Valley and Paradise Park
Manoa Road runs the entire length of Manoa Valley. At its south end is the Punahou School, built in 1841 for the children of the missionaries. Further up the valley, a left side road leads to the Waioli Tea Room, which is run by the Salvation Army, and was the model for Robert Louis Stevenson's 'Little Grass Shack'.

At the northern end of Manoa Road is Paradise Park, a 6ha (15 acres) garden set in a rainforest. Visitors can explore ancient Hau and bamboo trails and ethnic gardens. There are also hundreds of tropical flowers and birds. The internationally famous Dancing Waters and the entertaining Animal Quackers Duck Show are held here. Open daily 10am–5pm, entry fee is $7.50 adults, $6.50 juniors (13–17) and $3.75 children (4–12). For information ph 988 2141.

SOUTH-EAST OAHU

Hanauma Bay
Located in Koko Head Park, the Bay is an extinct volcano crater which has been flooded by the ocean. Legend says the volcanic action 10,000 years ago was caused when Pele, the Fire Goddess, made her last attempt to find a home on Oahu. The bay is a state marine conservation area. Consequently, no fishing is allowed, which makes for very friendly fish and excellent snorkelling. Elvis Presley fans will recognise the scenery from the movie *Blue Hawaii*.

Halona Blowhole
Best viewed from the lookout on Kalanianaole Highway near Koko
Head Crater. Miniature geysers are formed by the ocean forcing
through a tiny hole in the lava ledge.

Makapuu Beach
The most popular body-surfing beach on Oahu, Makapuu is out of
bounds for surf boards. The huges waves, however, can be deadly
in winter, and it is recommended that only experienced surfers
tackle them even in summer.

Sea Life Park
Located at Makapuu Point, Sea Life Park features an outstanding
display of Hawaii's exotic marine life in an oceanside setting. The
300,000 gallon Hawaiian Reef Tank is one of America's finest
aquariums, housing 2,000 island specimens: sharks, rays, moray
eels, turtles and exotic reef fish. The Park also has a bird
sanctuary, complete with albatrosses and a whaling museum.
Open daily 9.30am–5pm, entry fee $9.95 adults, $7.75 juniors
(7– 12) and $3.75 children (4–6). For information ph 923 1531 or
259 7933.

Waimanalo Beach
The longest continuous beach on Oahu 5km (3 miles), Waimanalo
has good surf for beginners in the arts of body and board surfing.
The northern end of the bay is part of the Bellows Field United
States Air Force Base, and is known as Bellows Beach. This part is
only open to the public on weekends and certain holidays.

Rabbit Island
Near Waimanalo, this is one of the many interesting islets that
border Oahu. The island looks like the head of a rabbit, and was
once overrun by them.

WINDWARD OAHU
Windward Oahu faces the trade winds, receiving heavy rainfall
throughout the year that produces forests and jungles.

Kailua
The beach here is good for swimming and windsurfing. The beach
park is divided into two by the Kaelepulu Canal.

Kaneohe
There are outstanding coral gardens in Kaneohe Bay, and glass-bottom boat tours leave from Heeia-kea Pier on Kamehameha Highway north of Kaneohe several times daily, ph 247 0375.

Haiku Gardens
This area was once a favourite haunt of the ancient Hawaiians, but now it is a jungle park with a restaurant overlooking grass houses, lily and tropical fish ponds and bamboo groves, ph 247 6671.

Byodo-In Temple
Japan's 900-year-old architectural treasure is duplicated in detail at the Valley of the Temples Memorial Park, beneath the cliffs of the Koolau mountains. The Oriental garden setting also has a carp pool, a 3m (9 ft) Buddha statue and a tea house. Open 9am–5pm, no entry fee, ph 239 8811.

Kualoa Regional Park
The beach here is narrow but long and sandy, and is a favourite picnic and swimming spot. From here there is a good view of the mountains and Kaneohe Bay. A few hundred metres offshore is the little island known to Hawaiians as Mokoli'i, but to others as Chinaman's Hat. Legend says that the goddess Hiiaka destroyed Mokoli'i (little lizard) and what can be seen today is all that remains of the lizard. At low tide it is possible to walk out and explore the island.

Sacred Falls
Off the highway near Hauula is a clear stream falling from sheer cliffs to the pool below. Lower falls drop over a 27m (87 ft) cliff. Legend has it that the falls are sacred to Kamapuua, the god of swine, who could change into a pig or a man at will.

Hauula Beach Park
There is a large walled-in swimming area here, but the main attraction for photographers, especially, is the beach hibiscus trees. During July and August the trees have yellow blossoms in the morning which gradually turn through the day to russet, then bright red then they fall off. Best seen in the morning, when there is a carpet of red flowers and trees covered in yellow.

Laie
Laie is a settlement of mainly Hawaiian and Samoan Mormons. About 2,400ha (6,000 acres) in this area have been a church project since 1864. They include the town of Laie, the Polynesian Cultural Center, a lodge and restaurant, a branch campus of Brigham Young University, and the Mormon Temple. This temple, built in 1920, is the first Mormon Temple to be constructed outside of Salt Lake City.

Polynesian Cultural Center
The Center is made up of native villages representative of those in Fiji, Tonga, New Zealand, Tahiti, Samoa, Marquesas and Hawaii. The 17ha (42 acres) advertises that it has been the number one visitor attraction for over 25 years. (I think that may be true if you don't count Pearl Harbour.) There are lagoons, waterfalls and lush tropical flora, and when the sun goes down there are Polynesian buffets and revues on an open air stage with a cliff backdrop and fountains for a curtain. The centre contains snack bars and a souvenir shop. Open Mon–Sat from 12.30pm. For information and reservations, ph 293 3333.

NORTH SHORE
The North Shore is the area between Kahuku Point, in the northeast corner of the Island, and Kaena Point, a rocky cape in the north-west. This is the part of Oahu that is famous for its surfing beaches, and where the championship surf meets are held.

Kahuku
The Kahuku Sugar Mill was in operation from 1890 until 1972, and although it no longer processes sugar cane it is the main feature of the village. It is now a complex of shops, a museum and displays, with a 'World of Sugar' tour.

Sunset Beach
A 3km sandy beach, averaging 60m wide, is one of the most famous and dangerous on Oahu, and the home of The Pipeline and Banzai Beach. Swimming in the summer, away from the lava rock outcrops is quite safe, but in the winter it is definitely inviting disaster.

Pupukea Beach Park

Here the coral reef causes a marvellous display of pounding surf in the winter, and forms the walls of tidal pools in the summer. A photographer's dream.

Puu o Mahuka Heiau

On a spur off Pupukea Road is the large ancient temple, which is a National Historic Landmark and State Monument. The walls are up to 158m (520 ft) long, and human sacrifices were made here. Legend says that a famous priest forecast that the Islands would be overrun by strangers from distant lands. From the temple there is a good view of Waimea Bay, inlet and beach park, and of the square stone belfry of St Peter's and St Paul's Catholic Mission Church.

Waimea Falls Park

A narrow canyon extending into the Koolau mountains, this was once a heavily populated Hawaiian village. Today, the 727ha (1,800 acres) site between Haleiwa and Kahuku is an unspoiled environment of tropical plant life, hiking trails and a lovely waterfall. The park is open daily 10am–5.30pm and there is normally an entry fee. Twice each month during the full moon, the Park opens its gates free to the public for 'Moonwalks', one-hour guided treks to the waterfall and back, offering an opportunity to experience life in an ancient Hawaiian valley at night.

Each year during the first weekend in October, the Makahiki Festival is held. This is a two-day celebration with dancing, games and arts and crafts.

For information ph 638 8511 or 923 8448. Take the No. 8, 9 or 20 bus from Waikiki and transfer to the No. 52 Circle Island bus at Ala Moana Shopping Center.

Waimea Bay

The original town of Waimea was destroyed by a flood in 1894, and now there are always more visitors than locals. The falls and park are the main attractions to most, but for experienced surfers the December and January tides with their 9–10m waves are the magnets. The official brochures say that swimming when surf is six feet or more is dangerous, which ensures that when the surfers are catching the waves there will be plenty of spectators.

Haleiwa

A mixture of old plantation and fishing village, Haleiwa was invaded by hippies in the late 60s and early 70s, but their arrival has not destroyed its charm as a pleasant village. Haleiwa Beach Park is one of the few beaches on the North Shore where swimming is safe all year round.

Liliuokalani Church

Also known as Waialua Protestant Church, the fifth sanctuary built on the old mission site. In the church is an ancient bell, a memorial archway, and a clock presented by Queen Liliuokalani in 1890, on which the letters of her name are used instead of numbers. The clock also has seven dials and seven hands indicating the months, days of the week, the week of the year, the day of the month, and phases of the moon.

Mokuleia

Once the site of a family ranch, this corner of Oahu is the home of the Dillingham Air Force Base. There are polo fields here which have enjoyed royal patronage over the years.

WESTERN OAHU

There are not a lot of tourist amenities on this side of the island, and the locals like it that way. Apart from the resorts of Makaha Valley, restaurants are scarce, and shopping centres specialise in food more than anything else.

If you want to visit Kaena Point, the most westerly point of Oahu, 4WD or sturdy hiking boots are essential as the Farrington Highway ends at Yokohama Bay and the track beyond goes through jagged wasteland.

Yokohama Bay Beach

A favourite surfing spot, the bay takes its name from the Japanese fishermen who tried their luck here.

Kaneana Cave

Near Makua just before the end of Farrington Highway, is the Kaneana Cave, named after the sharkman diety, who is supposed to have made his home in the cave.

Makaha
The Makaha Valley has the most developed resort area outside Waikiki, with hotel rooms, units, two 18-hole golf courses, tennis courts, manicured lawns and a heliport.

If you are just passing by, pop into the Resort and ask at the front desk for permission to visit the Kaneaki Heiau, an 18th century war temple that has been restored by the Resort and the Bishop Museum. The temple was dedicated to Lono, the god of agriculture, and was a place of prayer and human sacrifices.

Makaha Beach is the most famous on this coastline, and the International Surfing Championships have been held here since 1952.

Pokai Bay Beach Park
One of the few beaches where it is safe to swim all year, Pokai Bay is also one of the few safe places to anchor when the heavy surf is running. There is a good lookout point on the Barbers Point side of the bay, Ku'ilio'loa, with views of the coast from Makaha to Maili and of the Waianae Mountains.

CENTRAL OAHU
If you're coming from the north, first its sugar-cane fields, then it's pineapples, and more pineapples.

James Dole opened the first pineapple cannery in 1899, and today Hawaii produces about 45% of the world crop. On Kamehameha Highway is the Dole Pineapple Pavilion, where you can try the fresh fruit. They also have other snacks, souvenirs and gifts, and are open daily 9am–5pm. Ph 621 8408 for information.

Wahiawa
At the northern side of Whitmore Avenue, just before the town of Wahiawa, is a dirt track leading through fields to the Kukaniloko Birth Stones. It was here that the wives of ancient chieftains gave birth to their children, to the accompaniment of chanting and beating drums.

In the centre of Wahiawa (108 California Avenue) are the Healing Stones, which some folk still believe have healing powers. They are in a rough concrete shelter that could hardly be called a temple.

The Hongwanji Mission, 1067 California Avenue, has a Buddhist temple which has been carved from Japanese cypress and painted with gold leaf. A side entrance is usually open.

The Wahiawa Botanic Gardens, at 1396 California Avenue, has 4ha (9 acres) of plants that thrive in the cool, wet regions. Open daily 9am–4pm.

Schofield Barracks

When visiting the barracks you may have a feeling of deja vu, but relax, you probably have seen it before. It was here that *From Here To Eternity* and *Tora! Tora! Tora!* were filmed. Nearby is Kolekole Pass in the Waianaes, through which the Japanese flew to bomb Schofield and Wheeler Air Force Base.

The Tropic Lightning Museum, in the grounds of the barracks has weapons and artifacts from several wars. Open Wed–Sun, 10am–4pm, enter by the Macomb Gate on Wilikina Drive.

Mililani

The Catholic Church of St John, 95–370 Kuahelani, is worth a visit for its cement walls, granite altar, and sculptures depicting the Stations of the Cross. There are also bronze statues of the Virgin Mary and St John.

TOURS

Akamai Tours, Suite 1702, 17th floor, 2270 Kalakaua Avenue, Honolulu, ph 922 6485, offer the following:

1. *Deluxe Circle Island Tour:* 193km (120 miles) narrated tour around Oahu, with daily hotel pick-up at 9am returning at 5pm — $38 adults, $33 under 12, $27.50 under 7.

2. *5-0 Scenic Tour:* 97km (60 miles) narrated small circle island tour around the eastern end of the island and up into the rainforest behind Waikiki. Hotel pick-ups at 9am and 2.30pm, returning at 1pm and 6.30pm respectively — $19.50 adults, $17.50 under 12.

3. *Pearl Harbour/Punchbowl/City Tour:* 80km (50 miles) narrated city tour of Honolulu with a boat tour of Pearl Harbour including boarding the Arizona Memorial. Three tours daily with hotel pick-ups at 6.45am, 9am and 12 noon, returning at 11–11.30am, 1–1.30pm and 4.30–5pm respectively — $20 adults, $18 under 12

(children must be over 115cm (45″) tall to board the Arizona Memorial).

4.   *Polynesian Cultural Center Tours:* Scenic narrated drive along the Windward Coast of Oahu to the Cultural Centre. Two tours —Tour A picks up at 10.45am returning at 10–10.30pm — $56 adults, $34 under 12. Tour B picks up at 12.45pm returning at 10–10.30pm — $53 adults, $31 under 12.

5.   *Arizona Memorial Excursion:* Mini-bus tour to the Memorial and Visitor Centre. Three tours daily — $13 adults, $11 under 12 (please note height restriction above).

6.   *Waimea Falls Park, North Shore, Pineapple and Sugar Cane Fields Tour:* A five-hour tour through pineapple and sugar-cane fields to North Shore surfing beaches and Waimea Falls Park with visits to attractions on the way. Hotel pick-ups at 8.15am and 12 noon, returning at 1.30pm and 5.15pm — $27 adults, $24 under 12.

7.   *Honolulu Highlights:* A narrated city tour to include many of Honolulu's most popular and interesting scenic points. Three tours daily with pick-ups at 8.30am, 12.30pm and 4pm, returning at 11.30am, 3.30pm and 7.30pm — $14.50 adults, $12.50 under 12.

8.   *Sea Life Park Tour:* 97km (60 mile) narrated Small Circle Island Tour including admission and shows at Sea Life Park. Two tours daily with pick-ups at 8.30am and 1.30pm, returning at 12.30pm and 5.45pm — $25 adults, $21.40 under 12, $18 under 7.

9.   *Circle Island/Pearl Harbour Tour:* 193km (120 miles) narrated tour around the island with a boat tour of Pearl Harbour including boarding the Arizona Memorial. Hotel pick-up at 6.45am returning at 3.30–4pm — $31 adults, $28 under 12 (over 115cm).

10.   *Circle Island Snorkel and Picnic Tour:* Pick-up at 8am, returning at 5.30pm. Full day sightseeing tour including picnic lunch — $43 adults, $35 under 12, $29 under 7.

Akamai Tours can also arrange tours to the other islands.

Waikiki Trolley Tours, ph 526 0112. The Old Town Honolulu Trolley Tour is a nostalgic trip into Honolulu's past. The two-hour narrated tour includes unlimited on and off privileges for the day. Iolani Palace; Chinatown/Wo Fat; Academy of Arts; King

Kamehameha Statue; Mission Houses Museum; State Capitol; Hilton Hawaiian Village; Hawaii Maritime Center, Aloha Tower; Ward Centre; Royal Hawaiian Shopping Center; Restaurant Row — $7 all day pass. Also daily tours to Dole Cannery Square, Ala Moana Center, Ward Warehouse and Hilo Hattie.

E Noa Tours, ph 599 2561, have the following on offer:

1. *Circle Island Beach and Waterfall Adventure Tour:* Includes snorkelling at Hanauma Bay, with equipment and instruction provided, and lunch. Hotel pick-up at 8–8.15am returning at 5.30pm — $43 adults, $36 children 7–12, $30 children 6 and under.

2. *Royal Circle Island Tour:* Full day 193km (120 miles) tour with hotel pick-up at 9–9.15am returning at 5.30pm — $38 adults, $33 children 7–12, $27 children 6 and under.

3. *Pearl Harbour and Polynesian Cultural Center Circle Island Tour:* Escorted tour of the daytime activities at the Cultural Center. Hotel pick-up at 6.45–7am returning at 6pm — $43 adults, $27 children 5–11, $20 children 4 and under.

4. *Polynesian Cultural Center Royal Night Tour:* Scenic, narrated tour along the Windward Coast to the Cultural Center. Hotel pick-up at 12.30–12.45pm returning at 10.30pm — $57 adults, $31 children 5–11, free children 4 and under.

5. *Deluxe Little Circle Island Tour:* Half-day 97km (60 miles) tour, including Pali Lookout. Hotel pick-ups at 9–9.15am and 2–2.15am returning at 1pm and 6pm — $20 adults, $17 children.

6. *Honolulu City Tour:* Narrated, informative tour of the city including a magnificent view from atop Mt Tantalus. Hotel pick-ups at 8.30–8.45am and 2.30–2.45pm returning at 11.30am and 5.30pm — $15 adults, $12 children.

7. *Arizona Memorial Excursion:* Narrated 56km (35 miles) tour to Pearl Harbour including boarding the Memorial. Hotel pick-ups at 6.45–7am and 8.45 -9am returning at 10.30am and 12.30pm — $13 adults, $11 children over 115cm (45").

8. *Pearl Harbour and Honolulu City Tour:* Morning or afternoon 80km (50 miles) tour with pick-ups at 6.45–7am and 11–11.15am returning at 11.45am and 4pm — $21 adults, $18 children over 115cm (45").

9. *North Shore and Waimea Falls Park Tour:* Half-day excursion along Oahu's North Shore and a tour of Waimea Falls Park. Pickups at 8.15–8.30am and 12–12.15pm returning at 1.30pm and 5pm — $28 adults, $23 children 7–12, $21 children 6 and under.

Sun Tan Tours, ph 839 0944, offer the choice of travelling in a mini-bus or a stretch limousine, for the following tours:

1. *Circle Island Beach-Snorkel Picnic Tour:* All day tour includes snorkelling or beachcombing in Hanauma Bay including instruction and equipment. Departs 8am, returns 5.30pm — Mini-bus $41.50, limo $49.95.

2. *Pearl Harbour and Circle Island Tour:* 193km (120 miles) narrated tour including the new National Park Visitor Centre. Departs 7am, returns 4pm — Mini-bus $29.50.

3. *Pearl Harbour-Punchbowl City Cultural Tour:* 80km (50 miles) narrated tour. Departs 7am, returns 11.30am — $18.50 mini-bus, $24.50 limo.

4. *Mini Circle Island Tour:* 97km (60 miles) half-day tour of east Oahu. Departs 1pm, returns 5pm — $18.50 mini-bus, $24.50 limo.

SPORT AND RECREATION

Cruising and Sailing

Ani Ani Glass Bottom Boat Cruise. A one hour cruise off the shores of Waikiki, ph 947 9971.

Audacious Sail. Cruise including swimming, snorkelling and picnicking offshore Waikiki, ph 536 3641.

Bayside Divers. *Miller Time 111* sails out of Kaneohe Bay for inter-island cruises to Molokai and Lanai. Good amenities and scuba instruction is available, ph 235 4217.

Capt Bob's Picnic Sail. Catamaran *Barefoot* sails out of Waikiki to Kaneohe Bay for snorkelling, swimming, sailing, ph 926 5077.

Glass Bottom Boat. Catamaran *Holo Holo Kai* has full-day sailing trips, ph 536 3641.

Honolulu Sailing Co. Three sailboats fitted with underwater cameras, ph 235 8264.

Lotus Flower Sailing Adventures. A sailing ship patterned after the original *Mayflower*, 56 feet long complete with two private state rooms, ph 259 5429.

Tradewind Charters. Private and shared sailing with hands-on participation, ph 533 0220.

West Beach Sailing Company. Luxury yacht *Perfection* will take you on a trip you can design yourself. Private or shared charters available, ph 623 0965.

Fishing

Tradewind Charters. Deep Sea/Bottom Fishing. Marlin, ahi, mahimahi and ono can be caught all year round. Shared and exclusive charters available, ph 533 0220.

Golf

Kato's Golf Tours. Oahu's courses are often crowded. Kato's can guarantee a good day on a course of your choice. Package includes free transportation, green fees, cart, free use of golf clubs and shoes, ph 947 3010.

Hiking

Diamond Head Hikes. The Clean Air Team conducts hikes toward Diamond Head every Saturday and Sunday at 9am. Meet in front of the Honolulu Zoo, near the windsock, reservations unnecessary. Donation please. Bring a small flashlight.

Jet Skiing

South Pacific Watersports. Call 395 7626 and ask them to put a package together for you — a jet ski adventure coupled with one other water sport.

Parasailing

Aloha Parasail. Parasail the original way — no winches or bulky chairs. Be securely strapped into a padded harness, lifejack and parasail, then connected to a powerboat by a 300 feet towline. Free hotel pick-up and return, ph 521 2446.

Sea Breeze Parasailing. 'Fly' over Waikiki Beach in a free-flying harness, towed by an ocean-racing Scarab-boat, ph 486 9784.

South Pacific Watersports. Parasailing, jet skiing, water skiing and scuba and fast powerboating can all be arranged by them, ph 395 7626.

Scuba, Snorkelling, Snuba

Bayside Divers. 'Miller Time 111' sails with dive masters for beginners, novices or experts, ph 235 4217.

Blue Water Divers. Located at the Waikikian Hotel, ph 955 1066, they are experts, and will share their secrets with you.

Elite Dives. 15 years' experience in Hawaiian waters is yours in custom-dive boats, ph 637 9331.

Hawaii Snorkeling. Waikiki hotel pick-up and return provided to snorkel Hanauma Bay. Price includes mask, fins, snorkel, carry bag, fish food, ph 944 2846.

Honolulu Sailing Co. Only Coast Guard licensed, experienced skippers accompany these trips. Lunches can be provided, ph 235 8264.

Innerspace Odessy's Scuba. Dives at Shark's Cove and Three Tables on the North Shore. Half-day trips, ph 247 5409.

Leeward Dive Centre. Their custom-built 36 feet Radon has everything needed and they supply lunch, ph 696 3414.

South Seas Aquatics. Sunset, night and introductory dives, and underwater camera, on a 44 feet custom-built dive boat, ph 538 3854.

Waikiki Diving Center, 420 Nahua Street, ph 922 7188, and 1734 Kalakaua Avenue, ph 955 5151. One of the biggest diving shops on Oahu, specialising in private dives.

Skydiving

Parachutes in Paradise. Feel safe (I don't know how you could!) and secure skydiving in tandem. Over 20 years of parachuting experience, ph 637 8544.

Skydive Hawaii. Tandem jump with professionals at Mokulela, ph 521 4404.

Windsurfing/Sailboarding

Aloha Windsurfing. A member of the International Windsurfing Sailing Schools offering opportunities for novice or expert, ph 926 1185.

Kailua Sailboard. Beginners and experts on Kailua's safe beach, with all-day equipment rental plus transportation $40; with lessons $45. Rental only, $27 daily, $95 weekly. Beginners 3 hour lessons with gear only $35, ph 262 2555.

HAWAII — THE BIG ISLAND

The youngest island in the Hawaiian group, the Big Island is a land of contrasts. Larger in area than all the other islands combined, Hawaii has active volcanoes, snowcapped peaks, lush rainforests, monolithic cliffs and beaches of many colours.

It lies 193km (120 miles) south-east of Oahu, and is nicknamed 'The Orchid Isle' due to the profusion of these blooms, especially in the Hilo area.

The Big Island was the first to be settled by the Polynesians, and the first to greet the missionaries. Kamehameha the Great was born in Kohala (c. 1753) and ruled from Kailua, where he died in 1819. It was on this island in 1779, that Captain James Cook was killed at Kealakekua Bay.

HOW TO GET THERE

The Big Island is the closest gateway to Polynesia from Mainland United States, and has two major airports, at Hilo and Keahole-Kona. Both these airports are capable of accommodating wide-bodied jets.

Aloha and Hawaiian Airlines offer frequent daily inter-island flights. The flight from Honolulu to Hilo takes approximately 40 minutes, and that to Keahole-Kone, 30 minutes. The island of Maui is only a few minutes away by air.

There are also scheduled commuter and other air taxi services operating between islands.

TOURIST INFORMATION

Information offices are located at Suite 104, Hilo Plaza, 180 Kinoole Street, Hilo, ph 961 5797, and at 75 5719 W. Ali'i Street, Kona Plaza Shopping Arcade, Kailua-Kona, ph 329 7787.

There is a 24-hour, 7 day a week recorded message service called Volcano Update, ph 967 7977.

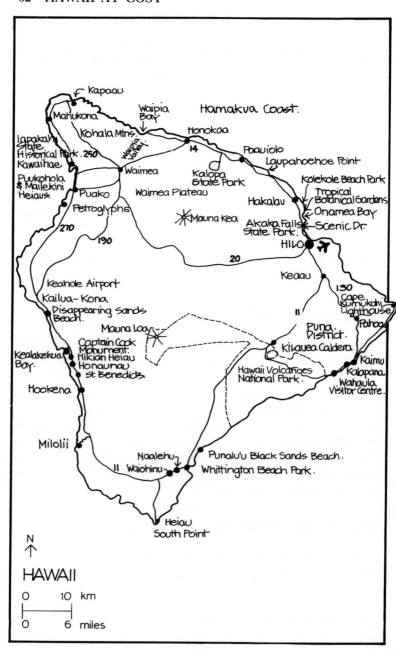

Kapaau
Mahukona
Waipia Bay
Kohala Mtns.
Hamakua Coast.
Honokaa
Lapakahi State Historical Park. 250
Kawaihae
Puukohola & Mailekini Heiaus.
Puako
Petroglyphs
270
190
Waipio Valley
Waimea
Waimea Plateau
Kalopa State Park
Mauna Kea
14
Paauilo
Laupahoehoe Point
Kolekole Beach Park
Tropical Botanical Gardens
Hakalau
Onamea Bay
Akaka Falls State Park.
Scenic Dr.
HILO
20
Keahole Airport
Kailua-Kona
Disappearing Sands Beach.
Mauna Loa
Captain Cook Monument.
Hikian Heiau
Honaunau
St. Benedicts.
Kealakekua Bay.
Hookena
Keaau
130
Cape Kumukahi Lighthouse
Pahoa
Puna District.
11
Kilauea Caldera
Hawaii Volcanoes National Park.
Kaimu
Kalapana
Wahaula Visitor Centre.
Milolii
Naalehu
Waiohinu
11
Punalu'u Black Sands Beach.
Whittington Beach Park.
Heiau
South Point

N

HAWAII

0   10 km

0   6 miles

ACCOMMODATION

The following prices for accommodation are for a standard double room per person per night, and should be used as a guide only.

Hilo
Hilo Hawaiian Hotel, 71 Banyan Drive, ph 935 9361 — $76; Hawaii Naniloa Hotel, 93 Banyan Drive, ph 969 3333 — $70; Hilo Bay Hotel, Uncle Billy's, 87 Banyan Drive, ph 935 0861 — apartments — $49–59; Waiakea Villas Hotel, 400 Hualani Street, ph 961 2841 — $40–45; Country Club Hotel, 11 Banyan Drive, ph 935 7171 — $35–42; Hilo Hukilau Hotel, 126 Banyan Drive, ph 935 0821 — $41; Dolphin Bay Hotel, 333 Iliahi Street, ph 935 1466 — $36.

Kawaihae
Mauna Lani Bay Hotel, P.O. Box 4000, Kohala Coast, ph 885 6622 — $295–325; Mauna Kea Beach Hotel, P.O. Box 218, Kamuela, ph 882 7222 — $220; Aston Shores at Waikoloa, Star Route 5200-A, Waikoloa, ph 885 5001 — condominium apartments — $155–210; Hyatt Regency Waikoloa Resort, One Waikoloa Beach Resort, ph 885 1234 — $195; Royal Waikoloan Hotel, P.O. Box 5000, Waikoloa, ph 885 6789 — $90–225; Parker Ranch Lodge, P.O. Box 458, Kamuela, ph 885 4100 — $58; Waikoloa Villas, Waikoloa Village Station, Kamuela, ph 883 9588 — condominium apartments — $70–85.

Kona
Kanaloa At Kona, 78–261 Manukai Street, ph 322 2272 — condominium apartments — $115–265; Hale Kai O Kona, Alii Drive — condominium apartments — $210; Kona By The Sea, 75–6106 Alii Drive, ph 329 0200 — condominium apartments — $125–155; Aston Royal Seacliff Resort, 75–6040 Alii Drive, ph 329 8021 — condominium apartments — $95–125; Kona Bali Kai, 76–6246 Alii Drive, ph 329 9381 — condominium apartments — $70–115; Kona Surf Resort Hotel, Keauhou-Kona, ph 322 3411 — $85–95; Kona Hilton Beach & Tennis Resort, 75–5852 Alii Drive, ph 329 3111 — $95; White Sands Village, 74–6469 Alii Drive, — condominium apartments — $85–95, Kona Islander Inn, P.O. Box 1239, ph 329 3181 — condominium apartments — $54–89; Hotel King Kamehameha, 75–5660 Palani Road, ph 329 2911 — $85;

Kona Reef, 75–5888 Alii Drive, ph 329 4780 — condominium apartments — $65–85; Keahou Beach Hotel, 78–6740 Alli Drive, ph 322 3441 — $70; Keauhou Resort Condominiums, 78–7039 Kamehameha III Road, ph 322 9122 — $50–62; Kona Magic Sands, 77–6452 Alii Drive, ph 329 9177 — condominium apartments — $55–62; Kona Bay Hotel Uncle Billy's, 75–5739 Alii Drive, ph 329 1393 — $59; Kona Seaside Hotel, 75–5646 Palani Road, ph 329 2455 — $48–58; Kona Mansions, Alii Drive, ph 329 4780 — condominium apartments — $52–55; Kona Tiki Hotel, P.O. Box 1567, ph 329 1425 — $35; Manago Hotel, P.O. Box 145, Capt Cook-Kona, ph 323 2642 — $29–32.

Volcano

Holualoa Inn, Mamalahoa Highway, Holualoa Village, ph 324 1121 — $75–85; Kilauea Lodge, P.O. Box 116, Volcano, ph 967 7366 — $65; Kalani Honua Conference Center and Retreat, RR2, Box 4500, Pahoa, ph 965 7828 — $36–58; Kilauea Volcano B & B, Old Volcano Hwy at Right Road, Volcano Village, ph 967 7216 — $40.

Ka'u

Seamountain at Punalu'u Colony 1, P.O. Box 70, Pahala, ph 928 8301 — condominium apartments — $63–83; Shirakawa Motel, P.O. Box 467, Naalehu, ph 929 7462 — $23–28.

LOCAL TRANSPORT

Bus

There are bus services between Hilo and Puna, Ka'u, Hamakua and Kona (via Honokaa and Waimea) at least twice a day and the fares are graded according to distance.

Hilo has a city bus service, (fare is 60c), and a shuttle bus operating between the hotels from 9am–2pm (also 60c).

For further information ph 935 8241. Bus timetables are available from the terminal in Mooheau Park.

Car

If you intend getting close to Mauna Loa, 4WD is mandatory, so if you don't want to join any of the tours on offer, you will need to hire a vehicle.

Canoe racing, 4th July, Oahu

Waikiki at dusk

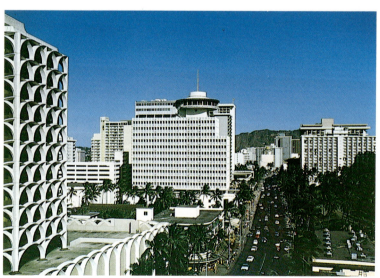

Kalakaua Avenue, Honolulu

The 'Arizona's' rusting ventilator and turret, Pearl Harbour

Young hula dancers

Rodeo at Makawao, Maui

There are nearly 50 car rental companies operating on Hawaii, so we will list only the majors:

Avis Rent-A-Car, General Lyman Field, Hilo, ph 935 1298/1290; Kona Station, P.O. Box 687, Kailua-Kona, ph 329 1745/1191.

Budget Rent-A-Car, P.O. Box 4938, Hilo Airport, Hilo, ph 961 0661; 74-5558-A Kaiwi Street, Kailua-Kona, ph 329 8511.

Dollar Rent-A-Car Systems of Hawaii, General Lyman Field, Hilo, ph 961 2101; Kona Airport, Kona, ph 329 2744.

Harper Car & Truck Rentals, 1690 Kamehameha Avenue, Hilo, ph 969 1478.

Hertz Rent-A-Car, Hilo Airport, Hilo, ph 935 2896; Kona Airport, Kailua-Kona, ph 329 3566; Kamuela Airport, Kamuela, ph 883 9400.

National Car Rental, General Lyman Field, Hilo, ph 935 0891; Kona Airport, Kailua-Kona, ph 329 1674.

Pacific Rent-A-Car, P.O. Box 4279, Hilo, ph 935 1936.

Roberts Hawaii, General Lyman Field, Hilo, ph 935 2858; Keahole-Kona Airport, Kailua-Kona, ph 329 1688.

Trac Systems Inc, 688 Kanoelehua Avenue, Hilo, ph 935 3385; P.O. Box 787, Kailua-Kona, ph 329 2437.

Tropical Rent-A-Car, Kona Hilton Hotel, Kailua-Kona, ph 329 1377.

United Car Rental Systems, Kona Airport, Kailua-Kona, ph 329 3411.

Distance and Driving Times
From Hilo to
  Kamuela — 88km (55 miles) — 1 hour 5 minutes.
  Hapuna — 117km (73 miles) — 1 hour 45 minutes.
  Kailua-Kona — 154km (96 miles) — 2 hours 15 minutes.
  Volcanoes National Park — 48km (30 miles) — 45 minutes.
  Kaimu Black Sand Beach — 48km (30 miles) — 45 minutes.

From Keahole-Kona Airport to
  Place of Refuge — 48km (30 miles) — 45 minutes.
  Kealakekua Bay — 42km (26 miles) — 1 hour.
  Kamuela/Waimea — 61km (38 miles) — 55 minutes.
  Hapuna Beach — 40km (25 miles) — 30 minutes.

Taxis
Readily available at the airport in Hilo, or ring from your hotel. Most taxis can be hired for touring, and have fixed rates for different areas.

EATING OUT AND ENTERTAINMENT

No one should ever go hungry on the Big Island, where there are plenty of restaurants offering every type of food imaginable. Again we have rated them according to price: expensive — $18 and over for a main course, moderate — $13–$17, inexpensive — $8–$12, budget $7 and under. Many of these places have live entertainment and you should check when making your reservations.

Hilo and Hamakua Coast
Capers, 235 Keawe Street, Hilo, ph 935 8801 — Italian, Continental — lunch Mon–Fri, dinner Mon–Sat — moderate.

Fiascos, Volcano Highway, near Banyan Drive, Hilo, ph 935 7666 — lunch, dinner from 11.30am every day — moderate.

Harrington's, 135 Kalanianaole Avenue, Hilo, ph 961 4966 — dinner from 5.30pm nightly — expensive.

Herb's Place Meals & Cocktails, Main Street, Honokaa, ph 775 7236 — open 5.30am–8.30pm Mon–Fri, 8am–8.30pm Sat —budget.

Hukilau Restaurant, 136 Banyan Way, Hilo, ph 935 4222 — breakfast and lunch daily 7am–1pm, dinner 4–8.30pm — moderate.

Reflections Restaurant, 101 Aupuni Street in the Hilo Lagoon Center, ph 935 8501 — lunch 11am–2.30pm, dinner 5–10pm daily — moderate.

Roussels, 60 Keawe Street, Hilo, ph 935 5111 — lunch 11.30am–4.30pm Mon–Fri, dinner Mon–Sat, 5–10pm — moderate.

Sun Sun Lau Restaurant, 1055 Kinoole Street, Hilo, ph 935 2808/2809 — lunch 10.30am–2pm daily, dinner 4–8pm Mon–Thurs, 4–9pm Fri–Sun — budget.

Ting Hao Mandarin Restaurant, Puainako Town Center, ph 959 6288 — lunch 10.30am–2.30pm daily, dinner 4–9pm Mon–Sat, 4.30–9pm Sun — inexpensive.

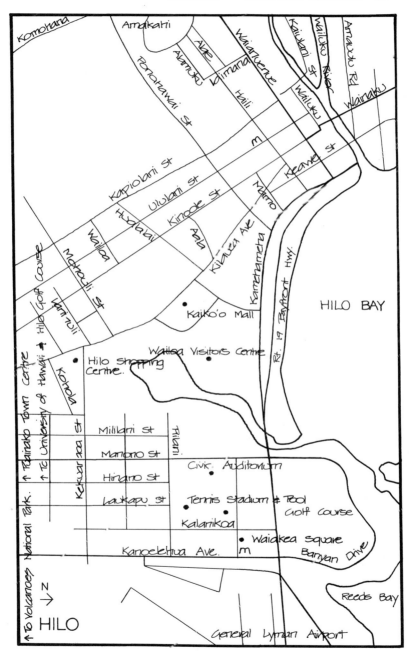

Uncle Billy's Fish & Steak Restaurant, Hilo Bay Hotel at 87 Banyan Drive, ph 935 0861 — breakfast 7–9am, dinner 6.30–8.30pm — hula show at 6pm every night — inexpensive.

Ken's House of Pancakes, cnr Banyan Drive and Kamehameha, ph 935 8711 — open 24 hours a day, 365 days a year — budget.

McDonald's, 177 Ululani Street, ph 935 9092 and Waiakea Kai, 88 Kanoelehua, ph 955 5743 — budget.

Zack's Famous Frozen Yogurt, Puainako Town Center, Volcano Highway, ph 959 2766 — 27 flavours! — budget.

Waimea/Kohala Coast

Bree Garden Restaurant, Kinohou Street, Waimea, ph 885 5888 — dinner 4.30–9.30pm nightly — moderate.

Cramped Quarters Cafe, Highway 19, Waimea/Kohala, ph 885 5066 — open 11am–7.30pm Mon–Sat — budget.

Don's Family Deli and Restaurant, Kapa'au, opposite King Kamehameha statue, ph 889 5822 — open 10am–8pm daily — inexpensive.

Harrington's Kawaihae, Kawaihae Center, ph 882 7997 — open nightly with live entertainmet Wed–Sat — moderate.

Hyatt's Legends of Polynesia, Hyatt Regency Waikoloa, ph 885 1234 — Mon, Wed and Fri — entertainment — expensive.

Mauna Kea Beach Hotel Buffet, Kohala Coast, ph 882 7222 — lunch noon–2.30pm — moderate.

Merriman's, Opelo Plaza, Waimea, ph 885 6822 — lunch Mon–Fri 11.30am–1.30pm plus Sunday Brunch, dinner 5.30–9pm nightly — moderate.

Royal Waikoloan, Kohala Coast, ph 885 6789 — Garden Cafe has sandwiches, salads and soups, etc, Royal Terrace has fresh seafood and Sunday Brunch — expensive.

Waikoloa Village Restaurant, on Village Golf Course, ph 883 9644 — open 7am–9pm daily — inexpensive.

Kona Coast

Burger King, 580 Kiluea Avenue, and 75–5597 Palani Road, Kona — open daily — budget.

Drysdale's Two, Keauhou Shopping Village, ph 322 0070 — daily 10am–2am — seafood and steaks — inexpensive.

Don Drysdale's Club 53, Kona Inn Shopping Village — open daily 11am–2am daily — light meals — budget.

Golden Bear Restaurant, Kaiwi Street, ph 329 7113 — open 11.30am–9pm Mon–Fri, cocktail service 5–9pm — budget.

Golden Chopstix, Kaahumanu Plaza, Highway 19 and Kaiwi Street, ph 329 4527 — inexpensive.

Fisherman's Landing, Kona Inn Shopping Village, ph 326 2555 — lunch 11.30am–2.30pm, dinner 5.30pm–10pm, to 10.30pm Fri and Sat — moderate.

Hotel King Kamehameha, 75–5660 Palani Road, Kona, ph 329 2911 — luaus Tues, Thurs and Sun 6pm — expensive.

Huggo's, Alii Drive, Kailua Bay, ph 329 1493 — lunch and dinner (BBQ ribs special Tues and Thurs) — moderate.

Hurricane Annie's, Kona Inn Shopping Village, ph 329 4345 — lunch 11.30am–4pm, dinner 4–9.30pm — Italian and Cajun — inexpensive.

Jameson's By The Sea, 77–6452 Alii Drive, ph 329 3195 — dinner Mon–Sat, lunch Mon–Fri — moderate.

Jolly Roger Kona Restaurant, Waterfront Row, ph 329 1344 — seafood — moderate.

Kanazawa-Tei Japanese Restaurant & Sushi Bar, 75–5845 Alii Drive, ph 326 1881 — inexpensive.

Keauhou Beach Hotel, 78–6740 Alii Drive, ph 322 3441 — buffets 5–9pm (seafood Fri–Sun, Chinese Mon–Thurs) — Sunday Champagne Brunch — moderate.

King Yee Lau, Kona Inn Shopping Village, ph 329 7100 — open 11am–9pm Mon–Sat, 4–9pm Sun — inexpensive.

Kona Chuckwagon Buffet, 75–6082 Alii Drive, ph 329 2818 — very American — budget.

Kona Ranch House, Kuakini Highway, ph 329 7061 — open daily from 6.30am — two restaurants in one — inexpensive.

La Bourgogne Restaurant, Kuakini Plaza South, Highway 11, ph 329 6711 — dinner 6–10pm Mon–Sat — reservations suggested — moderate.

Lanai's Siamese Kitchen, 74–5588 Pawai Place, ph 326 1222 — lunch 11am–3pm Mon–Fri, dinner 5–9pm Mon–Sat — budget.

McDonald's, 75–5729 Kuakini Highway, ph 329 7178, and 81–6655 Mamalahoa Highway, ph 322 3364 — budget.

Manago Hotel and Restaurant, Highway 11, Captain Cook, ph 323 2642 — breakfast 7–9am, lunch 11am–2pm Tues–Sun, dinner 5–7.30pm Tues–Thurs, 5–7pm Fri–Sun — budget.

Moby Dick's Restaurant, Hotel King Kamehameha, ph 329 2911 — dinner from 5.30pm nightly, Sun brunch 9am–1pm — moderate.

Pizzazz Pizza, Kaahumanu Plaza, cnr Highway 19 & Kaiwi Street, ph 329 2431 — lunch from 11am Mon–Sat — budget.

Poo Ping 2 Thai Cuisine, Kona Inn Village, ph 329 2677 — open 11am–8pm Mon–Sat — budget.

The Pottery Steak House in Pottery Terrace, cnr Walua Road and Kuakini Highway, ph 329 2277 — dinner from 6pm nightly — continental — moderate.

Rocky's Pizza, Lanihau Center, Kailua-Kona, ph 326 2734 and Keauhou Shopping Village, ph 322 3223 — open daily — budget.

Royal Jade Garden, Lanihau Center, ph 326 7288 — open 10.30am–10.30pm daily — Chinese — budget.

Sibu Cafe, Kona Banyan Court, Alii Drive, ph 329 1112 — open daily 11.30am–9pm — Indonesian — inexpensive.

Volcano National Park/South Point Area
Ka Ohelo Dining Room, Volcano House, Volcano National Park, ph 967 7321 — breakfast 7–10.30am, lunch 10.30am–2pm, dinner 5.30–9pm — moderate.

Kilauea Lodge, Volcano Village, ph 967 7366 — lunch 10.30am–2.30pm, dinner 5.30–9pm, closed Mon — continental — moderate.

Punalu'u Black Sands, Punalu'u, ph 928 8528 — continental — open daily 10.30am–8.30pm — inexpensive.

SHOPPING

Hilo/Hamakua Coast
Hilo Shopping Center, cnr. Kilauea Avenue and Kekuanaoa Street, has over 40 air-conditioned shops and restaurants. There is plenty of free parking.

Hawaiian Handcraft, 760 Kilauea Avenue, ph 935 5587, is open seven days a week, 9am–5pm, and specialises in handcrafted bowls made out of koa and other local woods. They also offer free guided tours of the workshop.

Hilo Hattie, 933 Kanoelehua Street, Hilo, ph 961 3077, have a large selection of swimwear, T-shirts and gifts. They also offer free guided tours of the establishment.

The Keawe Collection is a group of shops in Keawe Street, that are well worth a visit, particularly the Potters Gallery, cnr Keawe Street and Waianuenue Avenue, ph 935 4069, which has jewellery, raku and pit-fired pottery, paintings, wood work and other local handicrafts. Open 9am–5pm Mon–Sat.

Longs Drugstore has two locations — 555 Kilauea Avenue, ph 935 3358, and the Prince Kuhio Plaza, ph 959 5881. The stores are open daily, and there is ample free parking.

Woolworth in Prince Kuhio Plaza, Hilo, ph 959 4555, has literally everything for the shopping tourist. They also have a snack bar.

Honomu

The Crystal Grotto, Honomu Village, on the way to Akaka Falls, ph 963 6195, has a variety of quartz crystals and stones, island made wooden items, paintings and jewellery. Open daily 10am–5pm.

Akaka Falls Flea Market is next to Ishigo's General Store in Honomu. It specialises in everything Hawaiian, and is open daily 9am–5pm.

Honokaa

S. Hasegawa Ltd, Main Street, Honokaa, ph 775 0668, is a traditional country general store, with tropical fabrics, oriental gifts, toys, clothing, shoes, and cosmetics.

Hawaiian Holiday Macadamia Nut Factory, Route 19, halfway between Hilo and Kona, ph 775 7743. Here you can try free samples while watching the processing and packing of the nuts in the factory. They also have the company's own Kona coffee for sale. Open daily 9am–6pm.

Kama'aina Woods Inc is just off Main Street, Honokaa, ph 755 7722, and is open Mon–Fri 9am–5pm. Watch the skilled craftsmen fashion bowls, pot pounders, bracelets, etc out of koa, milo, mango and other native woods. A packaging and mailing service is available.

Waimea/Kohala

Parker Ranch Shopping Center, near the junction of Highways 19 and 190, has over 35 shops and restaurants and ample free parking.

Ackerman Galleries, Kapa'au (opposite the King Kamehameha statue) ph 889 5971, are open daily 9.30am–5.30pm. They have fine arts with a blend of original works of island artists, boutiques, Oriental antiques and primitive artifacts.

Lahaina Galleries, Mauna Lani Bay Hotel, Kohala, ph 885 7244, are open daily 9am–9pm, and feature works by such as Robert Lyn Nelson and Lau Chun.

Parker Square, Highway 19, Waimea/Kamuela, is Parker Ranch's newest shopping centre with 25 specialty shops and services, and ample parking.

Gallery of Great Things, Highway 19, Kamuela, ph 885 6171, is open daily 9am–5pm and has works by Island artisans from small koa boxes to koa furniture.

Kona Coast

Hilo Hattie, 75–5597A Palani Road, ph 329 7200, is open 7 days a week 8.30am–5pm, and offers the same range of clothing, gifts and tours as their other stores in Hawaii.

Kona Discount Mart 1 and 2. These two everything-under-one-roof shops are at 75-5691 Alii Drive, ph 329 6366, and 75-5663 Palani Road, ph 329 8214. They will also arrange to pack and mail your purchases for you.

Holliday Galleries, Kona Plaza Shopping Arcase, ph 329 0046, have original paintings by local artists, and limited edition bronze sculptures. They also stock collections of well-known artists, such as Frederick Remington. Open Mon–Sat 9am–5pm.

Lanihau Center, on Palani Road, Kailua-Kona, is the district's newest shopping centre and is a delight to visit for its scenic layout. There is unlimited free parking.

Kona Inn Shopping Village, 75–5744 Alii Drive, has over 50 specialty shops, restaurants and services. The Village is open daily 9am–9pm.

Keauhou Shopping Village, 78–6831 Alii Drive, on the corner of Kamehameha III Road, has 37 shops and services, and offers free shuttle service from Keauhou Hotels and Condos, ph 322 3500. The Village is open 7 days a week, Mon–Thurs, 9am–9pm, Fri, 9am–7pm, Sat, 9am–6pm and Sun 10am–5pm.

Lee Sands Wholesale Eelskin, Kona Marketplace, shop 1210, ph 329-2285 has one of the largest selections of exotic leathers and skins, such as sea snake, salmon and mink.

Kona Scenic Flea Market, on Halekii Street, off Highway 11, ph 329 5848. Open Thurs and Sat, 8am–3pm, and market has island products at very reasonable prices.

South Point/Punalu'u/Volcano
Hirano Store, 20 Mile on Volcano Highway, ph 968 6522, is open seven days a week — 5.45am–5pm Mon–Fri, 7am–5pm Sat, and 7am–noon Sun. The store has one of the best views of the erupting volcano from its ground floor, and stocks all the expected souvenirs.

SIGHTSEEING

HILO
The second largest city on the island and the capital, Hilo has a population of 42,000, and while not really a resort town, it does have its own charm, albeit often in need of a freshen-up. The waterfront has been hit twice by tidal waves, in 1946 and 1960, and in Laupahoehoe there is a monument to those killed in the 1946 disaster.

Banyan Drive
Most of the city's hotels are on Banyan Drive, which is lined with rows of these enormous trees, planted in the 1930s by visiting celebrities from all over the world.

Liliuokalani Gardens Park
Named after the last Hawaiian queen, the Park is 12ha (30 acres) of elaborate, authentic Japanese formal gardens. Situated on Banyan Drive.

Coconut Island
Quite close to the shore, Coconut Island was used by early Hawaiians for sacred birth and religious rituals.

Suisan Fish Auction
You have to be up early in the morning to catch this auction at Banyan Drive and Lihiwai Street, when the fishermen sell their catch.

Wailoa River and State Park
Off Kamehameha Avenue there are picnic areas surrounding Waiakea Fishpond, and the Wailoa Culture and Visitor Centre,

ph 961 7360. The park area was a busy business centre, but was twice destroyed by the tidal waves.

Lyman House Memorial Museum
To learn about the history and different cultures of the Big Island, and the early missionary days, a visit to Lyman House is a must. The house was built in 1839 and is at 276 Haili Street, ph 935 5021.

Naha Stone
On Waianuenue Avenue, which turns off Highway 19 (Kamehameha Avenue) is the famous Naha Stone which Kamehameha I overturned, fulfilling an ancient prophecy that whoever could do this would be king of the islands — shades of King Arthur!

Rainbow Falls
One of the most impressive falls in Hawaii, the Rainbow Falls are in Wailuku River State Park. Nearby are the Boiling Pots, a series of cascades falling from Mauna Kea into lava pools.

Kaumana Caves
8km (5 miles) from Hilo on Kaumana Drive are the Kaumana Caves, lava tubes formed during the eruption of Mauna Loa in 1881. Take care here as the terrain can be dangerous. From the area there are marvellous views of Hilo.

HAMAKUA COAST

Scenic Drive
11km (7 miles) north of Hilo on Highway 19 is the commencement of the 6km (4 miles) scenic drive leading to Hawaii Tropical Botanical Gardens at Onomea Bay. The 7ha (17 acres) gardens are a nature preserve and a sanctuary. Definitely a photographer's delight.

Alaka Falls State Park
Further along Highway 19 is the turnoff to Alaka Falls State Park, which has bamboo groves, ferns and orchids and the well-known Alaka Falls, which tumble 128m (420 ft) down a cliff face to the Kolekole Stream below. On the way to the Alaka Falls are the Kapuna Falls 122m (400 ft) which are almost as dramatic. The area has plenty of hiking trails, and there are rest-rooms and drinking fountains.

Beach Parks
There are several beach parks along the coast, including Kolekole, Waikaumalo and Laupahoehoe.

Laupahoehoe Point
Situated between the 21 and 22-mile markers, in Laupahoehoe, the point is the site of an elementary school and old settlement which were destroyed by the 1946 tidal wave. A monument has been erected here in memory of the 24 students and teachers who lost their lives in the disaster.

Paauilo
An old plantation town on a side road off the highway, Paauilo affords the visitor scenes from old Hawaii. There are a rusted, tumble-down sugar mill, tin roofed cottages and decrepit storefronts.

Kalopa State Park
On another side road to the west, the park is a lush forest and has camping grounds, cabins, picnic tables and restrooms. A good place for a stop for lunch.

Honokaa
The macadamia nut capital of the world, Honokaa is home to the Hawaiian Holiday Macadamia Nut Co, and the largest sugar mill in the world. The mill can process 4,000 tons of sugar cane a day, and because it uses cane waste as fuel it is almost totally self-sufficient.

The Hawaiian Holiday Macadamia Nut Co offer tours of their complex, and free samples in the retail store, ph 775 7743.

Honokaa is also an old plantation town, and many of the original buildings have been restored.

Waipi'o Valley
On Highway 240 is Waipi'o Valley, the Valley of the Kings. Historically and culturally important, it is 9km (6 miles) long and 1.6km (1 mile) wide, and is bounded on either side by lush, green cliffs 610m (2,000 ft) high. A favoured place of Hawaiian royalty, the once inaccessible valley can now be explored by guided tours. The Waipio Valley Shuttle, ph 775 7121, is a 1.5 hours jeep tour which includes great views of Hiilawe Falls.

WAIMEA/KOHALA COAST

Waimea

Waimea, also called Kamuela, is cowboy country, and home to what are claimed to be the world's largest independently owned cattle ranches. The famous Parker Ranch runs about 50,000 cattle on its 101,000ha (250,000 acres). The ranch was founded by John Parker, a sailor who jumped ship in 1809, and now has a Visitor Center and Museum, ph 885 7655. The museum includes a Duke Kahanamoku Room which will be of interest to sport fans.

In the town there are several historic churches, the Imiola Congregational Church, with its fine koa woodwork, having been built in 1857. There are also a few shopping centres, and at the corner of Highways 19 and 250 there is the Kamuela Museum, ph 885 4724, which has a fine collection of artifacts, though somewhat in disarray.

Kohala Mountains

Not far from the Kamuela Museum, Highway 250 heads north through the Kohala Mountains. Here the landscape changes as the road goes higher, with cactus, eucalyptus and lantana taking over the landscape. There are fantastic views down to the dry, black lava Kohala coastline.

Kapaau

Situated on Highway 270, Kapaau is the site of the original King Kamehameha I statue. Made in Florence in about 1879, this statue was lost at sea on the way to Hawaii, and found after a replica had already been installed in Honolulu. It was refurbished and sent to this area, the birthplace of the king.

Mookini Heiau

Off Highway 270, on the turnoff to the airport, is one of the island's most important temples in history, Mookini Heiau, believed to have been built about 480 AD. King Kamehameha's birthplace is further west along the same road.

Lapakahi State Historical Park

On Highway 270, south of Mahukona, the Park was once an ancient Hawaiian fishing village. Guided tours take visitors through the village, which has been reconstructed, giving an insight into ancient Hawaii, ph 889 5566.

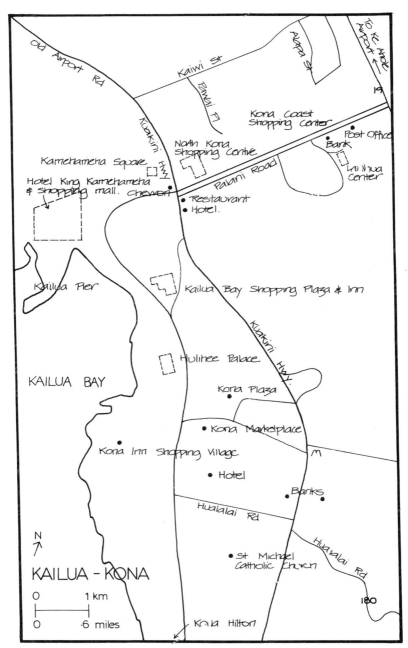

Puukohola Heiau

The temple, on Highway 19 near the end of Highway 270, was built by Kamehameha I in 1791 because a prophet said this would ensure his victory over the other island kings. He dedicated the temple to his war god by killing the last remining rival chief, probably ensuring the prophecy would come true.

Puako Petroglyphs

There are three sets of rock carvings here, and a well sign-posted route along the trail at the end of the road. These carvings are among the best in all the islands.

   The country between Puako and Kailua-Kona is lava crusted. There are views of Hualalai to the south, Mauna Kea to the east and Maui to the north. There are modern-day rock adornments along the way, where people have written their names among the black lava and white coral.

KAILUA

Originally a fishing village and first capital of the islands, Kailua is now jam-packed with hotels, restaurants and shopping malls.

Mokuaikaua Church

Situated on Alii Drive in the centre of town, the church is the oldest Christian place of worship on the islands. The first missionaries landed in 1820 and built this lava and coral building in 1836. The 34m (112 ft) steeple is a landmark and symbol for Kailua town.

Hulihee Palace and Museum

Situated directly across the street from the Mokuaikaua Church is the Hulihee Palace, which is now a museum, ph 329 1877. The two-storey building was the royal holiday home. There is an entrance fee.

Alii Drive

Alii Drive is the main street of Kailua-Kona and just about everything in the town is on this Drive. It then continues south from the town for about 8km (5 miles), passing Disappearing Sands Beach, also known as Magic Sands Beach, because the sand is seasonally washed out to sea leaving only black lava rocks, then it 'magically' returns.

St Peter's Catholic Church
On the rocky shore of Kahaluu Bay, St Peter's was built by the missionaries on a Hawaiian heiau. It is very small but the locals claim it is the world's second smallest church. (We don't know where the smallest is.)

Keauhou Bay
At the end of Alii Drive, the beautiful bay has plenty of resorts and several interesting historical sites. The Keauhou Beach Hotel will provide a map of the area showing the points of interest.

SOUTH KONA
Highway 11 crosses the slopes of Mauna Loa along the coffee belt. Pass through the small towns of Honalo and Kainaliu, with their friendly islanders, and arrive at Kealakekua, with its famous Little Grass Shack.

Kona Historical Society Museum
Close to the Grass Shack, the museum is filled with fascinating artifacts and memorabilia from the days of old Hawaii. Nearby are Mrs. Field Macadamia Nut Factory, the Honwanji Buddhist Temple, the Central Kona Union Church and the Lanakila and Christ Churches.

Captain Cook Monument
A white obelisk has been erected near the spot where Captain James Cook was killed in 1779. To get there go through the village of Napoopoo to Kealakekua Bay, and the momument stands on a distant shore. The best way to see it is to take one of the many boat cruises on offer that tour the bay. The cliffs behind the obelisk are riddled with Hawaiian burial caves.

Hikiau Heiau
A large lava structure on the shore nearby is the Hikiau Heiau, where Hawaiians once worshipped Cook as the god of Lono — one of the four major gods from Tahiti. Just before he was killed, Cook performed a Christian burial service for one of his crewmen in the temple.

Pu'uhonua O Honaunau
Translates as Place of Refuge, and was once a sacred sanctuary for defeated warriors or kapu breakers. It is now a national historic park and well worth visiting. There are free booklets for independent touring of the palace, heiaus and wooden idols found here.

There are two ways to get to the park — either by the unimproved road south from Kealakekua Bay, or via the main highway to the route 160 turnoff.

Wakefield Botanical Gardens
On the way from the Place of Refuge, the Gardens have spectacular tropical flowers and plants.

St Benedictine's Church
Situated up the hill from the Place of Refuge is St Benedictine's "Painted Church". The church's interior is a beautiful work of art by a Belgian priest who transformed the wooden chapel with murals of religious scenes. The grounds of the church have been the location for several Christmas television specials.

Highway 11 continues south past Hookena, passing over the 1919, 1926 and 1950 lava flows. About 48km (30 miles) from Kailua, there is a turnoff to Milolii, a vintage South Seas fishing village, with fascinating tidepools.

SOUTH POINT
Ka Lae (South Point) is the southernmost point of the United States. To get there follow Highway 11 to the South Point turnoff, then follow the narrow road about 19km (12 miles) to land's end and the lighthouse, where there are the remains of the oldest Hawaiian settlement in the Islands. Archaeological findings dating back to 750 AD include ancient canoe moorings set in solid rock. Ka Lae has the island's only green sand beach, made of volcanic olivine particles.

Kalalea Heiau
The temple stands on the tip of South Point, and offerings are still made here. The heiau is believed to hold a shark or other god over which prayers are offered.

Palahemo Well
Situated inland from the Kalalea Heiau is this well which was used by early settlers. Fresh water floats atop the salt water in a tidal pool. There are ancient petroglyphs (rock drawings) on the rim of the well.

Green Sands Beach
For the adventurous, or those with 4WD, there is a track along the shore for about 5km (3 miles) to Green Sands Beach.

Waiohinu
A small town on Highway 11 where there are the keikis (offshoots) of the monkeypod tree planted by Mark Twain in 1866. The original tree was felled by high winds. Nearby is the beautiful Kauaha'ao Church.

Naalehu
A small town, renowned for being the southermost community in the United States.

Whittington Beach Park and Punalu'u Black Sand Beach
Both parks have camping and picnicking facilities. At Punaluu archaeologists found ancient canoe moorings. The Ka'u Cultural Center, which is near the Black Sands Restaurant, has detailed information on the area, and also a spectacular mural painted by Herb Kane, a well-respected kamaaina artist.

Bird Park
Mauna Loan Road leads to the Bird Park which has one of the richest selection of Hawaii's native plants.

Volcanoes National Park
The most active volcanoes in Hawaii, Mauna Loa and Kilauea, are linked directly to the Pacific Plate's source of magma. A visit to the Kilauea Visitor Center, ph 967 7311, will give all the information and tips on viewing times, etc. that you need to fully appreciate the splendour of the park. Crater Rim Road features 18km (11 miles) of spectacular scenery, passing lava flows and steam vents in its circuit of Kilauea Crater.

Kilauea Iki Trail
Crater Rim Road takes the visitor to the Thurston Lava Tube, a 137m (450 ft) tunnel surrounded by ferns. The Kilauea Iki trail begins from the Thurston Lava Tube's parking area, and the two-hour hike offers views of Byron's Ledge, Kilauea Cauldera, Halemaumau fire pit and Puu Puai vent, before descending into the crater. Please take notice of the warning signs, and follow the path of piled lava pieces that mark the trail.

Devastation Trail
A half-mile walk in an area devastated by a 1959 cinder fallout. The pumice-covered landscape is covered with flowering plants, which makes an interesting contrast.

Halemaumau Crater

The firepit last erupted in 1982, and is the legendary home of Pele, the goddess of volcanoes. It is really a crater within a crater, being entirely contained within Kilauea.

Other attractions in the park include the Jaggar Museum, the Sandalwood Trail, and the scenic Chain of Craters Road.

Wahau'la Park Visitor Center and Museum

The center has information on a coastal walk in the direction of recent lava spills into the ocean. For information ph 967 7977, 967 7311. Behind the complex is Wahau'la Heiau, a temple built about 1250 AD. This is thought to be the last place where priests practised human sacrifice.

The road ends at a twenty-foot wall of lava. Several of the side roads are also severed by lava flows, so exit from the park means a backtrack of 45km (28 miles) along Chain of Craters Road.

PUNA

Volcano Village

Situated on the Old Volcano Highway, the village has small shops, snack bars and overnight accommodation in a rural setting.

Highway 11 passes through the townships of Glenwood, Mountain View and Kurtistown, with their many orchid nurseries. At Keaau, Highway 130 branches off to the east, and the Puna district. It links up with Highways 132 and 137 for a circuit route.

Kalapana

A black sand beach, studded with palm trees. The black sand is caused when molten lava reaches the sea and fragments. The ocean then grinds the black glass-like pieces into fine sand.

Star of the Sea Painted Church

Quite near Kalapana, this church is decorated with more of the folk art found in Kona's Painted Church. There is an ancient canoe ramp from which the Polynesians launched their outriggers.

Kaimu

Another black sand beach, which is much photographed, and probably the best known.

Cape Kumukahi Lighthouse
The lighthouse is situated on the state's easternmost point, and is
reached by a gravel road from the intersection of Highways 137 and
132. This entire area, apart from the lighthouse, was destroyed in
1960 when a lava flow swept through on its way to the sea. To give
an idea of the size and strength of the flow, it actually added about
455km (500 yards) of land to the island. Next to the lighthouse
stands an ancient Hawaiian Heiau.

TOURS

Hilo Bay Air, Commuter Air Terminal, General Lyman Field,
ph 969 1545 or 969 1547, are open 8am–5pm with 24-hour telephone service. They have a wide range of tours, and specialise in
comprehensive volcano tours.

'Io Aviation, Hilo General Lyman Field, ph 935 3031 are open
9am–6pm daily. They have narrated scenic tours in helicopters
and airplanes. They have a combined Hilo/Volcano tour at very
competitive rates, and also offer big game hunting helicopter
tours.

Big Island Air have the only two-hour island flightseeing tour,
with commentary by the pilot. For reservations phone their
24-hour line at Kona Airport, 329 4868. They also have Hawaii's
only jet charter service.

Kona Helicopters, ph 329 0551, have narrated tours in jet
helicopters, and serve all resorts.

Kenai Air, have trips to Mauna Loa, the Hamakua Coast,
Kilauea Crater, or a Mauna Loa/Kilauea combination. For reservations phone Hawaii 245 8591, Kauai 329 7424.

Koa Air Services, Kona Airport, ph 326 2288, have narrated tours
of Kona-Kohala in Cessna high wing airplanes.

Hawaii Airventures, Keahole Airport, ph 329 0014, have circle
island/volcano tours.

Akamai Tours, ph 329 7324, have Visit a Neighbour Island tour
which includes return airfare with Aloha Airlines, 24-hour use of a
Dollar Rent A Car, and the hotel of your choice.

Roberts Hawaii, have Great Escapes tour packages to other
islands including airfares, room and car hire. Prices per person (to
be used as a guide only) are: Ohau — $82; Molokai — $85; Maui
— $90; Kauai — $93, ph 329 1688 in Kona, or 935 2858 in Hilo.

Atlantis Submarine, ph 329 6625. Kona based, the submarine tour lasts one-hour and goes to depths of up to 100 ft. This is a unique way to see the coral reefs and marine life. Children under 4 not permitted on this tour.

Papillon Helicopters, ph 885 5995, have personalised tours that take you anywhere you want to go on the Big Island, including the Captain Cook Monument and the City of Refuge.

Parker Ranch Tours, ph 885 7655 for information and reservations. They have Paniolo No. 1 Country tour daily 9am–1pm and noon–4pm — $38 includes lunch, and Paniolo No. 2 Shuttle Tour, every 20 minutes for 1.5 hour tour — $15.

Glassbottom Boat — 1 hour rides. Day ph 933 0025, after 6pm ph 322 3102. Departs daily from Kailua Pier at 9.30am, 11am, 1pm, 2.30pm and 4pm. Cap't Bob's Kona Reef Tours original glass bottom boat crosses over into shallow, fish-filled waters. You can even feed the fish.

Hilo Hattie have tours of their garment factory and showroom, complete with fashion shows and pareau demonstrations. In Hilo they are at 933 Kanoelehua Street, ph 961 3077, and in Kona 75–5597A Palani Road, ph 329 7200.

SPORT AND RECREATION

Golf

Kona Country Club, 9.5km (6 miles) south of Kailua-Kona on Alii Drive, ph 322 2595. Open daily, starting times required. 27-hole course. Green fees — 18 holes — Kona Surf guests $45, Kona residents $53, non residents $75.

Waikoloa Village Golf Club, midway between Highways 19 and 190, ph 883 9621. The course was designed by Robert Trent Jones, Jr and is a challenge to the serious golfer. Call for tee times, Randall Carney, PGA, Director of Golf. Green fees — 18 holes — $47.

Waikoloa Beach Resort Golf Course, near the Royal Waikoloan Hotel on the Kohala Coast, ph 885 6060. 18-hole course. Call for tee times, Dennis Rose, PGA, Director of Golf. Green fees — 18 holes — Royal Waikoloan guests $55, non-guests $90.

Mauna Lani Resort's Francis H. I'i Brown Golf Course, South Kohala, ph 885 6655. Jerry Johnston is the director of golf. Green fees — 18 holes — guest $50, non-guest $100.

Mauna Kea Golf Course, Mauna Kea Beach Hotel, Kawaihae, ph 882 7222. J.D. Ebersberger is the director of Golf. Starting times required one day in advance. Green fees — 18 holes — guest $40 (plus $30 for cart), non-guest $75 (plus $3 — for cart).

Volcano Golf and Country Club, Hawaii Volcanoes National Park, ph 967 7331. A unique course in a volcano. Green fees — 18 holes — $25 daily, with a local driver's licence, $28 daily without.

Sea Mountain Golf Course, Punalu'u, ph 928 6222. A championship course. Green fees — 18 holes — $41 daily.

Discovery Harbour Golf and Country Club, Waiohinu, ph 929 7353. A very scenic course. Call for green fees.

Horseback Riding

Horseback Riding and Mounting Fishing Adventures, Waiono Meadows, Holualoa, ph 329 0888, have a guided 2-hour trail ride, or a combination 4-hour horseback riding and fresh water fishing. The ride is through lush green meadows on the slopes of Mt Hualalai overlooking the Kona Coast.

King's Trail Rides O'Kona, ph 323 2388. Leave from Kealakekua Ranch Center, near Captain Cook. Experienced guides will assign you to the appropriate tour and horse. Camping trips are available.

Ironwood Outfitters Mountain Trail Rides, at Kohala Ranch in the Kohala Mountains, ph 885 4941. Rides on the privately owned 16,160ha (40,000 acres) working cattle ranch.

Scooter Hire

Rent Scootah, Rawson Plaza behind Big Island Toyota, Kailua-Kona, ph 329 3250, have brand new automatic Honda Sprees and Gyros Scooters for rent. Hourly and daily rates with multi-day discounts. Call for a free shuttle in the Kona area. Valid driver's licence required.

Fishing Charters

Sea Wife Charters, P.O. Box 2645, Kailua-Kona, ph 329 1806. Captain Tim Cox is the master of the 42 feet *Sea Wife*. All tackle included. Trips depart from Kailua Pier, 7.30am and 12 noon Mon–Sat. Marlin charters available.

Red Wave Sportfishing, P.O. Box 4736, Kailua-Kona, ph 329 4056. Marlin charters with experienced captain and crew.

Lucky Lil Sportfishing. Moored at slip D–10, Honokohau Harbour, ph 325 5438 (24 hours). The *Lucky Lil* is a zero tolerance vessel and the captain is Captain George Wilkins, a marlin specialist.

Gold Coast Sportfishing on *Medusa*, ph 329 1328 (day), 329 0164 (evenings). The tournament winning yacht will chase marlin, tuna, wahoo and mahimahi, or light tackle trips for ulua, barracuda, skipjack and amberjack can also be arranged. They can also arrange combination fishing and diving trips.

Kamalii Kai, ph 329 4163 after 6pm, is a 44 feet striker with twin dependable diesels and a wide beam to make fishing spacious and comfortable. Exclusive charters are offered by Captain Kai, an island-born skipper.

Twin Charter Sportfishing, ph 325 6374. Captains Larry and Gary Pries are US Coast Guard-licensed and insured and their 35 feet *Janet B* can be chartered for a full or a half day, up to six anglers. Lunches and beverages are included with the charter.

Howdy Do Sportfishing, P.O. Box 4532, Kailua-Kona, ph 328 9101. The 28 feet Tollycraft has shaded cabin, bridge and is tournament equipped for the novice or experienced angler. Split-boat and three-quarter day trips available.

Omega Sport Fishing, P.O. Box 5323, Kailua-Kona, ph 325 7859 or 325 7593. Captain Klaus offers fishing charters for special low rates when booking directly with him. Sharing is available, and all tackle and ice are provided.

Sportfishing on *The Panic*, ph 329 1948 or 329 5802 (reservations for evenings). Captain Bobby Henriques offers challenging sportfishing in Kona waters. 30 years' experience in these waters. Families and children are welcome.

Trojan Sea Raider Charter Fishing, Honokahau Harbour, ph 325 7840. Captain Bob White guarantees you will catch fish aboard his 34 feet deluxe yacht.

Scuba Charters

Sea Paradise Scuba, Keauhou Bay, ph 322 2500. Close to all Kona Hotels with easy dockside parking. Morning, afternoon and sunset/night dives available.

Kona Aggressor, Kailua-Kona, ph 329 8182. Open Mon–Fri 9am–5pm. Charters for novice to expert divers.

King Kamehameha Divers, 75–5660 Palani Road in Hotel King Kamehameha Mall, ph 329-KONA. Open daily 7.30am–6.30pm. Professional instructors available, and underwater video service and camera rentals.

Maalaea Harbour

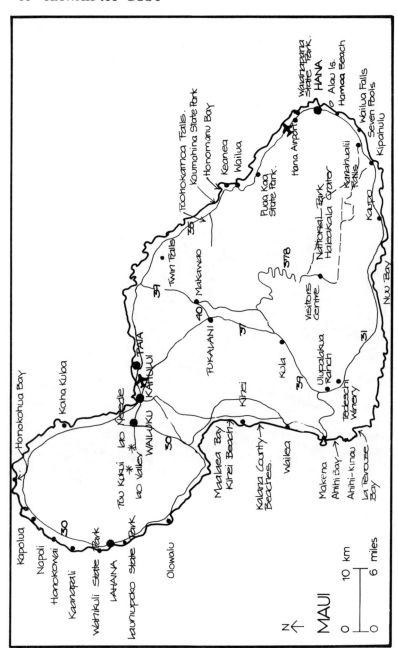

MAUI

N

0 ___ 10 km
0 ___ 6 miles

MAUI

Geologists say that the island of Maui was formed by volcanic eruptions beneath the sea over long periods of time, the islanders have a different idea of its formation.

Legend says that the demi-god Maui created all the islands when one day his fishhook caught up the oceans bottom. It was Maui who snared the sun and forced it to slow its passage, allowing the Hawaiians more time to fish and grow taro.

Whichever theory you wish to believe, Maui, or the Valley Isle as it is called, is a splendid island in the Pacific, with blue-green mountains, sun-drenched beaches, hidden coves and many waterfalls.

Maui was the site of a great victory in battle by King Kamehameha I, and the south-west coast was the playground of the Alii, the Hawaiian royalty.

The second largest of the Hawaiian Islands, Maui has an area of 1,880km^2 (729 sq miles) and is 113km (70 miles) south-east of Oahu.

HOW TO GET THERE

Aloha Airlines and Hawaiian Air offer frequent daily flights from Honolulu (25 minutes), and there are scheduled commuter and other air taxi services operating between the islands.

Maui is also served directly from Mainland USA by United Airlines and American Airlines, and charter flights of trans-Pacific air carriers.

There are two airports on Maui, the main one at Kahului, and small one at Hana.

TOURIST INFORMATION

The Hawaii Visitors' Bureau visitor information office is at 380 Dairy Road, Kahului.

ACCOMMODATION

Finding somewhere to stay in Maui is not a problem, but it is always wise to book ahead. The following prices are per person per night in twin share accommodation.

WEST MAUI

Lahaina

Maui Marriott Resort, 100 Nohea Kai Drive, ph 667 1200 — $195–230; Sheraton Maui Hotel, 2605 Kaanapali Parkway, ph 661 0031 — $185; Aston Sands of Kahana, 4299 Honoapiilani Highway, ph 669 0400 — $159–229; Embassy Suites Resort at Kaanapali, 104 Kaanapali Pl, ph 661 2000 — $175; The Westin Maui, 2365 Kaanapali Parkway, ph 667 2525 — $175; Napili Kai Beach Club, 5900 Honoapiilani Road, ph 669 6271 — $140; Royal Lahaina Hotel, 2780 Kekaa Drive, ph 661 3611 — $130; Kahana Villa, 4242 Honoapiilani Highway, ph 669 5613 — apartments — $110–205; Aston Kaanapali Shores, 3445 Lower Honoapiilani Highway, ph 667 2211 — $129–169; Papakea Beach Resort, 3543 Honoapiilani Highway, ph 669 4848 — apartments — $104–117; Hale Mahina Beach Resort, 3875 Lower Honoapiilani Road, ph 669 8441 — apartments — $100; Kaanapali Royal, 2560 Kekaa Drive, ph 667 7200 — $125–170; Maui Kaanapali Villas, 2805 Honoapiilani Highway, ph 667 7791 — apartments — $109–139; Hono Koa, 3801 Lower Honoapiilani Road, ph 669 0979 — apartments — $90–130; Paki Maui, 3615 Lower Honoapiilani Highway, ph 669 8235 — apartments — $99–119; Hololani Resort Condominium, 4401 Lower Honoapiilani Road, ph 669 8021 — apartments — $88–125; Lahaina Shores Hotel, 475 Front Street, ph 661 4835 — apartments — $87–94; Honokeana Cove, 5255 Lower Honoapiilani Road, ph 669 6441 — apartments — $85; Hale Kai, 3691 Honoapiilani Road, ph 669 6333 — apartments — $80; Hoyochi Nikki, 3901 Lower Honoapiilani Road, ph 669 8343 — apartments — $80; Kulakane, 3741 Lower Honoapiilani Road, ph 6696119 — $80; Makani Sands, 3765 Honoapiilani Road, ph 669 8223 — apartments — $80; Nohonani, 3723 Lower Honoapiilani Road, ph 669 8208 — apartments — $76–82; Maui Kai Condominium, 106 Kaanapali Shores, ph 661 0002 — apartments — $75–105; Kaleialoha Condo, 37–85 Honoapiilani Highway, ph 669 8197 — apartments — $69; Noelani Condominium Resort, 4095 Lower Honoapiilani Road, ph 669 8374 — apartments — $65.

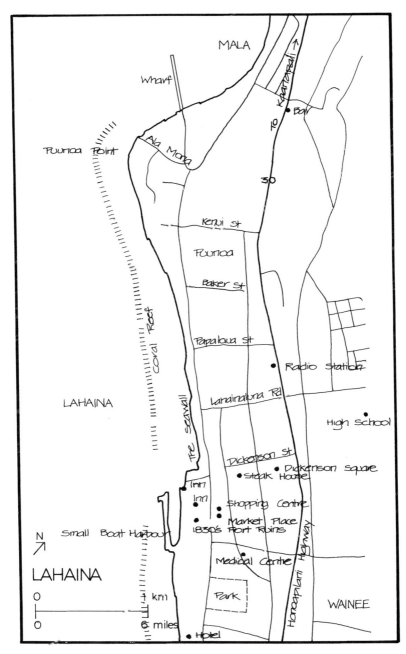

MALA

Wharf

TO Kaanapali →

Puunoa Point

Ala Moana

Bar

30

Coral Reef

Kenui St

Puunoa

Baker St

Papalaua St

Radio Station

Lahainaluna Rd

LAHAINA

High School

The Seawall

Dickenson St

Dickenson Square

Steak House

Inn

Inn

Shopping Centre

Market Place

Small Boat Harbour

1830's Fort Ruins

Medical Centre

N

Honoapiilani Highway

LAHAINA

Park

WAINEE

0 ———1 km

0 ———6 miles

Hotel

Kaanapali
Hyatt Regency Maui, Kaanapali Beach Resort, ph 661 1234 —
$195; Kaanapali Alii, 50 Nohea Kai Drive, ph 667 1400 —
apartments — $180–245; Kaanapali Beach Resort, 2525 Kaanapali
Parkway, ph 661 0011 — $115; Mahana At Kaanapali, 110
Kaanapali Shores Place, ph 661 8751 — apartments — $119–139;
Whaler at Kaanapali Beach, 2481 Kaanapali Parkway, ph 661 4861
— apartments — $90–95.

Kapalua
Kapalua Villas, One Bay Drive, ph 669 5656 — apartments —
$250–375; Kapalua Bay Hotel, One Bay Drive, ph 669 5656 —
$185–205.

Napili
Napili Point, 5295 Honoapiilani Highway, ph 669 9222 — apart-
ments — $129–179; Napili Shores Resort, 5315 Honoapiilani
Highway, ph 669 8061 — apartments — $105–130; Coconut Inn,
181 Hui Road, ph 669 5712 — $75–90; Napili Sunset, 46 Hui
Drive, ph 669 8083 — $77; Napili Surf Beach Resort, 50 Napili
Place, ph 669 8002 — apartments — $64–120; Napili Village
Hotel, 5425 Honoapiilani Highway, ph 669 6228 — $65–75.

SOUTH MAUI
Kihei
Maui Prince Hotel, 5400 Makena Alanu Road, ph 874 1111 —
$180–280; Makena Surf Resort, 96 Makena Ala Nui Road, ph 879
1331 — apartments — $165–270; Maui Hill, 2881 S. Kihei Road,
ph 879 6321 — apartments — $115–145; Kamaole Sands, 2695 S.
Kihei Road, ph 879 0666 — apartments — $110–170; Aston
Kamaole Sands, 2695 S. Kihei Road, ph 879 0666 — apartments —
$105–150; Luana Kai, 940 S. Kihei Road, ph 879 1268 —
apartments — $110–120; Comfort Suites Hotel, 2259 S. Kihei
Road — $89–129; Maui Vista, 2191 Kihei Road, ph 879 7966 —
apartments — $89–109; Kamaole Nalu, 2450 Kihei Road, ph 879
1006 — apartments — $85–110; Kihei Beach Resort, 36 S. Kihei
Road, ph 879 2744 — apartments — $78–101; Hale Pau Hana,
2480 S. Kihei Road, ph 879 3778 — apartments — $75–105;
Laulea Maui Beach Club, 980 S. Kihei Road, ph 879 5247 —
apartments — $75–110; Sugar Beach Resort, 145 N. Kihei Road,
ph 879 2778 — apartments — $65–100.

Mana Kai-Maui, 2960 S. Kinei Road — hotel — $77–85; Leina'ala, 998 S. Kinei Road, ph 879 2235 — apartments — $75–85; Maui Lu Resort, 575 S. Kihei Road, ph 879 5881 — hotel — $68–98; Kihei Surfside Resort, 2936 S. Kihei Road, ph 879 1488 — apartments — $63–98; Hale Kamaole, 2737 S. Kihei Road, ph 879 2778 — apartments — $55–87; Kealia Condominium, 191 N. Kihei Road, ph 879 0952 — $55–75; Kihei Alii Kai, 2387 S. Kihei Road, ph 879 6770 — apartments — $55–75; Kihei Kai, 61 N. Kihei Road, ph 879 2357 — apartments — $50–75; Shores of Maui, 2075 S. Kihei Road, ph 879 9140 — apartments — $50–70; Kihei Akahi, 2531 S. Kihei Road, ph 879 2778 — apartments — $45–70; Nani Kai Haie, 73 N. Kihei Road, ph 879 9120 — apartments — $45–70; Lihi Kai Cottages, 2121 Iliili Road, ph 879 2335 — $42–54; Wailana Sands, 25 Wailana Place, ph 879 2026 — $35–55.

Maalaea
Makani A Kai Condominium Rental, R.R. Box 389, Maalaea Village — $65–90; Hono Kai Resort, R.R. Box 389, Wailuku, ph 244 7012 — apartments — $55.

Wailea
Stouffers's Wailea Beach, 3550 Wailea Alanui, ph 879 4900 — resort — $185–285; Maui Inter-Continental Wailea, P.O. Box 779, ph 879 1922 — hotel — $145–175; Wailea Villas, 3750 Wailea Alanui, ph 879 1595 — apartments — $100–120.

CENTRAL MAUI
Kahului
Maui Beach Hotel, 170 Kaahumanu Avenue, ph 877 0051 — $62–68; Maui Seaside Hotel, 100 West Kaahumanu Street, ph 877 3311 — $54–62.

EAST MAUI
Hana
Hana Bay Vacation Rentals, P.O. Box 318, Hana, ph 248 7727 — private homes and cottages — $80; Hotel Hana-Maui, P.O. Box 8, Hana, ph 248 8211 — on Hana Bay — $360 (full board).

LOCAL TRANSPORT
Bus
Bus services on Maui are limited. There is a service from Wailea to Kapalua, stopping in Malaea, Lahaina and Kaanapali, seven days a

week. There is also a shuttle service between the hotels and Whaler's Village at Kaanapali Beach.

Car
There are plenty of car rental companies on Maui, the better known ones having offices at the Airport. Others who have their offices in the towns will sometimes arrange for pick-up at the airport, but you pay for the privilege. Be sure to check your insurance coverage, and beware that some companies do not allow their cars on the road around the West Maui Mountains, or the road around the south-east side of the island from Hana. Here are a few names and addresses:

Avis Rent A Car, Kahului Airport, ph 871 4471 or 871 7575; Kaanapali, 10–3 Halawai Street, Lahaina, ph 661 4588.

Budget Rent A Car, Kahului Airport, ph 871 8811.

Dollar Rent-A-Car Systems of Hawaii, Kahului Airport, ph 877 2731.

Hertz Rent A Car, Kahului Airport, ph 877 5167.

Kihei Holidaze Rentals, 1979 South Kihei Road, Kihei, ph 879 1905.

Pacific Rent A Car, Kahului Airport, ph 877 3065.

Practical & Atlas Car Rental, P.O. Box 126, Puunene, ph 871 2860.

Roberts Hawaii, Kahului Airport, ph 87 6226.

Sunshine Rent-A-Car, Dairy Road, Kahului, ph 871 6222.

Trac Systems, Inc., 41 Hana Highway, Kahului, ph 836 0788.

Tropical Rent-A-Car, 41 Hana Highway, Kahului, ph 877 0002; 20-A Halawai Drive, Lahaina, ph 661 0061.

United Car Rental Systems, Kahului Airport, ph 871 7328 or 523 2095.

Distance and Driving Time
From Kahului Airport to

Kahului — 5km (3 miles) — 5 minutes.

Wailuku — 10km (6 miles) — 10 minutes.

Kihei (Post Office) — 14km (9 miles) — 20 minutes.

Lahaina — 43km (27 miles) — 45 minutes.

Kaanapali — 48km (30 miles) — 50 minutes.

Haleakala (summit) — 60km (37 miles) — 1 hour 30 minutes.

Hana — 84km (52 miles) — 2 hours 30 minutes.

Kapalua — 58km (36 miles) — 1 hour.

Wailea — 29km (18 miles) — 35 minutes.

EATING OUT

WEST MAUI

Lahaina

Lahaina Steak 'N Lobster, 1312 Front Street, Lahaina, ph 667 5558 — American — open breakfast, lunch and dinner — moderate.

Marie Callender's, Lahaina Cannery, ph 667 7437 — American — open breakfast, lunch and dinner — moderate.

Old Lahaina Cafe, 505 Front Street, Lahaina, ph 667 1998 — American — open lunch and dinner — moderate.

Mr. Sub, 129 Lahainaluna Road, Lahaina, ph 667 5683 — American — open lunch — budget.

Bettino's, 505 Front Street, Lahaina, ph 661 8810 — Continental — open breakfast, lunch and dinner — moderate.

Longhi's, 888 Front Street, Lahaina, ph 667 2288 — Italian — open breakfast, lunch and dinner — expensive.

Village Pizzeria, 505 Front Street, Lahaina, ph 661 8112 — Italian — open lunch and dinner — budget.

Old Lahaina Luau, 505 Front Street, Lahaina, ph 667 1998 — Hawaiian — open dinner — moderate.

Kobe Steak House, 136 Dickenson Street, Lahaina, ph 667 5555 — Oriental — open dinner — moderate.

Kaanapali

Cafe Kaanapali, Whalers Village, Kaanapali, ph 661 0946 — American food — open breakfast, lunch, dinner — moderate.

H.S. Bounty Restaurant, Whalers Village, Kaanapali, ph 661 0946 — American food — open breakfast, lunch and dinner — inexpensive.

Sound of the Falls, Westin Maui, Kaanapali, ph 667 2525 — Continental — open dinner — moderate.

Swan Court, Hyatt Regency, Kaanapali, ph 661 1234 — Continental — open breakfast and dinner — expensive.

The Rusty Harpoon, Whalers Village, Kaanapali, ph 661 2123 — Continental — open breakfast, lunch and dinner — moderate.

Ricco's Old World Deli, Whalers Village, Kaanapali, ph 661 4433 — Italian — open lunch and dinner — budget.

Spats, Hyatt Regency, Kaanapali, ph 661 1234 — Italian — open dinner — moderate.

Drums of the Pacific, Hyatt Regency, Kaanapali, ph 661 1234 — Hawaiian — open dinner — moderate.

Chico's Cantina, Whalers' Village, Kaanapali, ph 667 2777 — Mexican — open lunch and dinner — moderate.

El Crab Cracker, Whalers Village, Kaanapali, ph 661 4423 — Seafood — open lunch and dinner — moderate.

Lahaina Provision Co., Hyatt Regency, Kaanapali, ph 661 1234 — Seafood — open lunch and dinner — moderate.

Leilani's on the Beach, Whalers Village, Kaanapali, ph 661 4495 — Seafood — open dinner — moderate.

Villa Restaurant, Westin Maui, Kaanapali, ph 667 2525 — Seafood — open dinner — moderate.

Kahana

Kahana Keyes, Valley Isel Resort, Kahana, ph 669 8071 — American — open dinner — moderate.

Erik's Seafood Grotto, Kahana Villa Condominium, ph 669 4806 — Seafood — open dinner — moderate.

Kapalua

Pineapple Hill, above Kapalua Bay Hotel, ph 669 6129 — Continental — open dinner — moderate.

Kapalua Bay Club, 900 Kapalua Bay Drive, ph 669 8008 — Seafood — open lunch and dinner — moderate.

SOUTH MAUI

Kihei

Kihei Seas, Rainbow Mall, Kihei, ph 879 5600 — American — open dinner — moderate.

Jesse's Luau Polynesia, 1945 S. Kihei Road, ph 879 7227 — Hawaiian — open dinner — moderate.

Erik's Seafood Broiler, 2463 S. Kihei Road, ph 879 8400 — Seafood — open dinner — moderate.

Kihei Seas, Rainbow Mall, Kihei, ph 879 5600 — Seafood — open dinner — budget.

Makena

Price Court, Maui Prince Hotel, Makena, ph 874 1111 — American — open dinner — expensive.

Kamehameha the Great, Kohala, Hawaii

Township of Wailuku, Maui

Seven pools, Maui

Haleakala Crater, Maui

Iolani Palace, Oahu

Opaekaa Falls, Kauai

Maalaea
Buzz's Wharf, Maalaea Harbour, ph 661 0964 — Seafood — open dinner — moderate.

CENTRAL MAUI

Kahului
Rainbow Room, Maui Beach Hotel, Kahului, ph 877 0051 — American — open breakfast, lunch and dinner — budget.

East West Room, Maui Palms Hotel, Kahului, ph 877 0071 — Oriental — open dinner — budget.

Red Dragon Room, Maui Beach Hotel, Kahului, ph 877 0051 Oriental — open dinner — moderate.

Wailuku
Mark Edison's Restaurant and Lodge, in Iao Valley, ph 242 5555 — Seafood — open lunch and dinner — moderate.

EAST MAUI

Casanova Italian Deli, 1188 Makawao Avenue, ph 572 0220 — Italian — open breakfast, lunch and dinner — moderate.

Poli's, 1202 Makawao Avenue, ph 572 7808 — Mexican — open lunch and dinner — moderate.

ENTERTAINMENT

Most of the hotels have a laua at least once a week, others have them more often. For example, The Hyatt Regency on Kaanapali Beach has its "Drums of the Pacific" revue Mon, Tues, Wed, Fri and Sat in their outdoor theatre. The Luau show begins at 5.30pm — adults $40, children (6–12) $32, infants (5 and under) free. They also have a Cocktail Show beginning at 7.15pm — adults $24, minors (20 and under) $21.

We will presume you have tried a Mai Tai in Honolulu, after all it's almost obligatory, so now you can experience a Maui Tai. Blackie's Bar have dreamt up this one, but beware, it may be even more lethal than the original. Blackie's is on Highway 30 between Lahaina and Kaanapli, ph 667 7979, and they advertise they have the coldest beer on Maui. You can also get tacos, burritos, enchiladas, nachos and burgers, and they have live entertainment Mon, Wed, Fri and Sun, 5–8pm.

SHOPPING

WEST MAUI

Shopping Centres

505 Front Street, next to the Lahaina Shores Hotel, has over 45 shops, including art galleries, boutiques, and beach-front restaurants. The centre is open seven days a week 9am–9pm (6pm Sun) and has plenty of free parking. Ph 667 2514 for information.

Lahaina Cannery Shopping Center, between Lahaina and Kaanapali Beach, is built on the site of the original pineapple cannery, and has over 50 shops and restaurants. Open daily 9.30am–9.30pm, the centre has free parking.

Whalers Village, Kaanapali Beach, also has over 50 shops and restaurants, with a free trolley service daily from 9am–11pm with departures every thirty minutes.

Hilo Hattie, 1000 Limahana Place, Lahaina. Open daily 8.30am–5pm, including holidays and weekends. There is a free bus which leaves the flagpole opposite the Courthouse in Lahaina 7 times a day. This shop stocks an enormous range of aloha, resort and swim-wear.

Koala Blue, 844 Front Street, Lahaina, ph 661 7000, has Australian inspired styles in cool 100% cotton, and stocks everything from T-shirts and sweats to jackets and blouses.

Lahaina Galleries has four locations — 117 Lahainaluna Road, ph 661 0839; 728 Front Street, ph 667 2152; the Kapalua Gallery at Kapalua Bay Resort, ph 669 0202; and Gallery Kaanapali in Whalers Village, ph 661 5571. The galleries feature the works of artists Robert Lyn Nelson, Guy Buffet, Americo Makk and Hisashi Otsuka, and others. Open 9am–9pm daily.

Larry Dotson Gallery has two shops in Lahaina — 143 Lahainaluna Road, ph 661 3838; Pioneer Inn (Hotel Street), ph 661 7197. Both feature the works of Robert Lyn Nelson and Pegge Hopper, Larry Dotson and Japan's Otsuka. They also have lithographs, prints, posters and wood carvings. Open Mon–Sat 9.30am–9pm and Sun 11am–9pm.

CENTRAL MAUI

Aloha Lei Greeters, 520 Keolani Place, Kahului, have fresh tropical leis, proteas, anthuriums, coconut hats, certified tropical plants to carry home. Ph 877 7088 for information about mail order delivery of fruit and flower baskets. Open daily 8.30am–6.30pm.

Mai Swat Meet, Kahului Fairgrounds, off Puunene Avenue, Highway 35. Every Sat and Sun, 8am–1pm, hundreds of stalls display crafts, souvenirs, jewellery, antiques, art, shells and other bargain-priced items. Admission — adults 50c, children under 12 free, ph 877 3100.

SIGHTSEEING

WEST MAUI

Olowahu Beaches
On route 30, 10km (6 miles) south of Lahaina, there are beaches north and south of Olowalu General Store. The surfing is good about half a mile north of the store.

Launiupoko State Park
5km (3 miles) south of Lahaina, near the West Maui Mountains, is Launiupoko State Park. The beach is good for fishing, but not for swimming.

Puamana Park
A good place for a picnic with excellent views, about 3km (2 miles) south of Lahaina.

Lahaina
Kamehameha the Great made this his capital in 1795, after conquering Oahu, Kamehameha III had his capital here, and it remained the capital of the Islands until 1845.

When the missionaries arrived in 1823, they were shocked at the attitudes and carryings-on of the natives and the sailors who visited in their whaling ships. The Congregationalists put a stop to the licentious behaviour, but not before there was a battle royal with the sailors, in which the mission homes were attacked with cannons.

The Lahaina of today is an interesting town, filled with sites and scenes of great interest to students of Hawaiian history and legend.

Carthaginian II is a steel-hulled schooner docked in the harbour, and now a museum of the old whaling days. There is an entrance fee.

The Pioneer Inn on Wharf Street was built in 1901, and just north of this is the Hauola Stone, a chair-shaped stone which the ancient Hawaiians believed had healing powers.

The Banyan Tree in front of the courthouse, was planted in 1873, and is said to be the largest in all Hawaii.

The Courthouse was originally built as a palace for King Kamehameha III, and relocated here in 1859. There is an art gallery in the basement. On either side of the courthouse are the ruins of the old fort, built in the 1830s.

The Baldwin Home, the oldest building in Maui, is on Front Street. Built out of coral and stone in the early 1830s for the Rev Dwight Baldwin, a medical missionary, the house is now a museum, ph 661 3262. There is an admission fee.

Waiola Cemetery and Church are both on Wainee Street. The cemetery has graves dating back to 1823, and the church was the site of the first Christian services held on Maui.

Hale Paahao, is also on Wainee Street, and is an old gaol built for the drunken and disorderly members of the whaling crews, in 1854.

Lahainaluna School, up the hill on Lahainaluna Road, was established by missionaries in 1831, and is the oldest school west of the Rocky Mountains. The first building of poles and grass was replaced by a stone building which still stands. From the school there is a superb view of Lahaina.

Hale Pa'i, Lahainaluna Road, is a printing house which still has the quaint old press on which Hawaii's first newspaper was printed in 1834.

Lahaina Jodo Mission, about half a mile north of Lahaina on Ala Moana Street, is a Buddhist complex with a temple and pagoda. Here is the largest ceremonial bell in Hawaii, and a giant bronze Buddha.

Maluulu o Lele Park is a good swimming beach on Front Street, near Whalers Market.

Lahaina Beach is north of Lahaina town on Puunoa Place, and is the best beach in Lahaina.

Wahikuli State Park

Located on Route 30 between Lahaina and Kaanapali, the park has picnic areas and restrooms, and there are tennis courts opposite. The swimming is very good, but surfing is poor.

Kaanapali

North of Lahaina, on Route 30, Kaanapali is a town full of hotels and condominiums. Hanakaoo Beach Park has good swimming on both sides of Hanakaoo Point. The white sandy Kaanapali Resort Beaches are all along Route 30. They have good views to Molokai and Lanai, and although often very crowded, are well worth a visit. Around Black Rock at the Sheraton Maui Hotel, there is very good swimming, body-surfing and skin diving.

Napili

Napili also has its share of hotels and condos, but it also has Napili Bay Beach with excellent swimming and snorkelling. But be warned that the currents can become hazardous when the surf is high.

Kapalua Beach (Fleming Beach)

One of the most picturesque and safest swimming beaches on Maui also has great snorkelling. It's about 11km (7 miles) north of Kaanapali, off Highway 30.

Honokohau Bay

Near here Highway 30 becomes Highway 34, and the road hugs the coastline high above the ocean in between sandstone cliffs. A little further along the road is not sealed and becomes a mass of potholes and ridges, but for the stout-hearted the scenery is very picturesque.

Kahakuloa

Visiting this village, in a valley beside a deep bay, is like stepping back in time. The little wooden houses are protected from the wind by the headland rising from the sea, and the people live, and raise their cattle, much the same as their ancestors did.

Puu Kukui

After Kahakuloa, the 1,764m (5,788 ft) Puu Kukui dominates the scenery.

Halekii Heiau

North of the town of Kahului on a side road, are the remains of ancient temples of worship, sacrifice and refuge, ordered to be destroyed by King Kamehameha II in 1819. Heiau has now been partially restored.

SOUTH MAUI

The coastline from Maalaea Bay to Makena is one beautiful beach after another, making this area a favourite holiday destination. The road follows the coast from Kihei to La Perouse Bay, but the last stretch from the 1790 lava flow to the Bay, is practically 4WD territory.

Maalaea Bay

It is from Maalaea Bay that the Pacific Whale Foundation have cruises to 'spot the whales'. Every year North Pacific humpback whales journey south from Alaska to breed in the warm waters of Hawaii. They usually arrive around November and stay until June. The largest of these giants measure about 14m (45 ft) and weigh up to 40 tonnes. They feed only in the polar regions, building up an extremely thick coat of blubber, off which they live during their time in Hawaii. A point of interest — the whales don't have teeth, but rather horny bone plates that hang from the upper jaw and form a sieve-like mat, netting small animals. More information on the cruises is found under the section 'Tours'.

Kihei Beach

Stretching from Maalaea Bay to Kihei, the beach is accessible from the highway along its entire length. It is not really a swimming beach, but good for jogging. There are picnic tables and rest-rooms at Kihei Memorial Park, near the centre along the beach. As with all the beaches in this area, afternoon winds can be a real problem.

Kalama County Beach Park

Situated on South Kihei Road across from Kihei town, Kalama is not a very good swimming beach, and the outlying reefs cause shallows. There are picnic facilities.

Kamaole Beach Parks

Three parks in all, with lovely green lawns, trees and best of all, good for swimming. Same problem as all the others with the afternoon winds.

Wailea

A deluxe 606ha (1500 acres) beachfront resort, owned by Alexander & Baldwin, with facilities including two hotels, condominiums, restaurants, two championship 18-hole golf course, a tennis club, and five excellent beaches with views of neighbouring islands. The resort is three times the size of Waikiki.

Makena

One of Maui's best and most beautiful beaches, and not as commercially developed as some. Once it was a haven for hippies, but the Seibu Corporation of Japan has built a 404ha (1,000 acres) resort and the area has gone up-market.

Ahihi-Kinau Reserve

A fascinating land and ocean reserve of over 808ha (2,000 acres), with lava flows, tidepools and coral reefs which protect numerous species of fish and coral.

La Perouse Bay

La Perouse Bay and Ahihi Bay were once one and the same. Then Haleakala erupted in 1790 and the lava flow formed Cape Kinau, dividing the bay into two. La Perouse Bay takes its name from the French explorer who anchored here in 1786, prior to his last fatal trip.

CENTRAL MAUI

The commercial and civic centres of Maui are in the adjoining towns of Kahului and Wailuku.

Kahului

A busy harbour town, with a population of around 15,000, Kahului has plenty to offer the shopper, but not much for the sightseer. There's nothing to entice the surfer either, and the beaches in this area have extremely strong currents, and definitely not for the faint-hearted.

Kanaha Pond Wildlife Sanctuary

Situated on Highway 32, the Sanctuary was once a royal fishpond, but now it is a bird refuge, with particular emphasis on the rare Hawaiian stilt.

Wailuku

The county seat of Maui, Wailuku is at the foothills of the West Maui Mountains, and is an interesting old town. It has a woodfront section, off Market Street, called Happy Valley — so named because it was once the red-light district, not because of the disposition of its inhabitants.

Iao Valley
The valley is a tranquil park now, but was the site of a bloody battle in 1790 when Kamehameha conquered Maui in the famed Battle of Kepaniwai.

Kaahumanu Church is the oldest church on Maui, having been built in 1837, and was named for Maui-born Queen Kaahumanu.

Hale Hoikeike is the Maui Historical Society museum, in the Bailey Mission Home, built in 1841. It has an interesting display of early missionary items and Hawaiian artifacts, ph 244 3326.

About 2km down the road is Kepaniwai Heritage Gardens, a country park with Chinese and Japanese pavilions, a taro patch and thatched hut, several arched bridges, a swimming pool and an oriental garden.

Iao Needle
After Haleakala Crater, the Iao Needle is probably Maui's most famous landmark. The mountain is a 686m (2,250 ft) high cinder cone, and Maui's most-visited attraction.

EAST MAUI
The Hana Highway (36) between Kahului and Hana, is one of the most scenic drives in Hawaii. The road is very windy, and although it is only about 84km (52 miles) between the two places, the drive will take from 2.5 to 3 hours.

Paia
Only 11km (7 miles) east of Kahului is the quaint little town of Paia, and this is where the twists and turns in the road commence, as it winds past sugar cane fields, across gorges, through valleys and along fern covered hillsides.

Twin Falls
Just off the main road, about 32km (20 miles) from Kahului, Twin Falls has a swimming hole which is a welcome visiting place if the weather is hot.

Puohokamoa Falls
There is a picnic area here, beside a large pool — a perfect spot for a picnic lunch.

Honomanu Bay
On a dirt road east of Kaumahina State Park, about 48km (30 miles) from Kahului, is a beautiful black sand beach. Unfortunately, there are no facilities here, but it's a great spot for surfing, though often too rough for swimming.

Keanae Arboretum
It's worth a stop here to walk through the beautiful tropical gardens, and just past this spot there is left turn onto the road to the peninsula. From the point there are great views of Haleakala. On the way there are rustic houses and a coral-and-stone church, which is not open to visitors.

Wailua
A lush agricultural and fishing village with a lookout that has a choice view of the entire Keanae peninsula and the coastline.

Puaa Kaa State Park
The name means "the place of the rolling pigs", which dates from the days when pigs were said to have rolled down the hills in this area. The park has a picnic area and waterfall.

The are a lot of side roads leading to lookouts with spectacular views of the coastline — if you have time, why not try them all?

Waianapanapa State Park
Here there is a lava tube which you can walk through to the edge of a black-sand beach. Nearby there is a blowhole, and off the shore are several arches. Strong swimmers and scuba divers, by diving into a pool and swimming underwater, can reach a big inner cave, a legendary trysting place for lovers of old.

Hana Bay
Affectionately known as "Heavenly Hana", the town looks out over the bay. Because of the high rainfall in this area the countryside is lush and green with developed agriculture. In the town there is a plaque commemorating the birthplace of Kaahumanu, King Kamehameha I's favourite wife, who had a lot to do with the overthrow of the ancestral Hawaiian religious system.

The best view of the town is from Mount Lyons, the camel shaped hill with the cross.

Hana Cultural Centre, on Uakea Road, has an interesting display of Hawaiian artifacts and antique photographs.

Hamoa Beach

Reached by a side road several kilometres south of Hana, Hamoa is a privately owned beach. The uninhabited island just off shore is called Alau Island.

Wailua

At Wailua Gulch there are two large falls, Kanahualii and Wailua Falls, which cascade down the cliff faces. Ohe'o Stream, not far away, is better known as Seven Pools, because a series of falls tumbles into seven large pools, which are rock-bound and some provide good swimming holes. From here there is an extremely good view of the surrounding rugged coastline.

Charles Lindbergh's Grave

2km (1.2 miles) past Seven Pools there is the Palapala Hoomau church, and in the yard is the grave of Charles Lindbergh, the famous avaitor. Lindbergh spent his last days in the area, and chose to be buried in this quiet, serene place.

Kaupo

There is not much to this little town of tin-roofed dwellings, but just above the town is Kaupo Gap. Through the Gap billowing clouds pour into Haleakala Crater.

Nuu Landing

There are ancient village ruins here among a lava and scrub landscape. Further along the road, which veers away from the coast are ancient petroglyphs.

Ulupalakua Ranch

Now we are back into country of lush vegetation, and the nearby Tedeschi Winery, the only winery in Hawaii, gently beckons. It is well-known for its light pineapple wine, a forerunner to the production of grape wine from vineyards on the slopes of Haleakala. The winery was originally an old gaol, built in 1857.

Also nearby are the ruins of the Makee Sugar Mill which dates back to 1878.

Kula Botanical Gardens

The Gardens are on Route 377 which branches off Highway 37 just before the octagonal church called the Church of the Holy Ghost (built in 1897). They have an aviary, pond, a Taboo Garden of poisonous plants, and many different species of protea. There is an admission fee to the gardens, ph 878 1715.

Makawao
A small town which will you make you feel you are in the middle of the wild, wild west of the United States of a bygone era. They even hold a rodeo every July 4.

The town is the starting point for two tours. The first follows Olinda Road (Highway 39) past Pookela Church, built in the 1850s, through the Tree Growth Research Area, on past Olinda Nursery and the University of Hawaii Agricultural Station back to Makawao.

The second takes Highway 40 to the Hana Highway, through the town Haiku, then circles back to Makawao.

Haleakala National Park
It was here, according to Polynesian legend, that the demigod Maui captured the sun and held it to give his people more daylight hours. And it is here that you can stand and capture an unforgettable scenic memory. From the crater's topmost rim to its floor is a drop of 914m (3,000 ft). The floor measures 65km^2 (25 sq miles), a fascinating area of richly coloured cinder cones. Haleakala's last eruption was more than 200 years ago. A public observatory stands on the rim of the volcano's crater. The outer wall of the volcano, cut by ravines and gullies, slopes down to the shore of the island.

SNORKELLING, DIVING AND SAILING

Cruises departing from Lahaina Harbour
Maui Princess departs daily at 7am, and cruises to Molokai, The 118 feet luxury ferry is met by an island guide for a day of sightseeing, a Hawaiian-style beach party and barbecue, and a horse-drawn wagon ride. Ph 661 8397 for reservations and information.

Genesis is a luxury yacht with a roomy cockpit, wide beam and recessed deck. It sails on half-day sail/snorkel tours with lunch, and romantic sunset dining tours for only 9 couples with serenaded starlight sailing, ph 667 5667. The starlight cruise starts at $56 per person, including meal.

Seabern Yachts, ph 661 8110, have morning and sunset whalewatch trips daily on their 42 feet luxury yachts. Six persons maximum, from $29 per person.

Whale Sail take 15 passengers maximum on their 40 feet catamaran *Kamehameha* for a sunset Whale Sail — $24 adults, $18 children, or a noon Whale Sail & Snorkel, including gear, instructions and free use of underwater camera — $34 adults, $24 children. Refreshments and snacks on all sails, ph 661 4522 for reservations and information.

Lucky Strike Charters offer deep sea trolling, light tackle bottom fishing and share boat or private charters, ph 661 4606.

Daily Whalewatch provide a champagne sunset sail aboard their Santa Cruz 50 *Scotch Mist* — $29. They also offer morning or afternoon sailing, snorkelling and exploring the coral gardens including gear, instruction, drinks and snacks — $39. Ph 661 0386, 667 9089.

Glassbottom Cruise aboard the Chinese Junk *Lin Wa* — fully narrated. Departs 9.45am, 11.45am, 1.15pm and 2.45pm, ph 661 3392.

Lanai Picnic/Snorkel Sail on a fast multi-hulled sailing yacht. Luncheon sail — $39; afternoon sail and snorkel — $25; 2.5 hour whalewatch — $20 (children under 12 ($15). All sails include fresh pineapple, Maui chips, beverages, snorkel gear and instruction, ph 661 3047.

Trilogy Excursion have tours on three sailing multi-hull yachts, *Trilogy 1*, *Trilogy 11*, *Trilogy 111* to Lanai. Departs daily 6.30am returning approx. 4.30pm — adults $125 + tax, children $62.50 + tax, ph 661 4743. They also have whalewatching cruises Jan-April.

Pardner is a 46 feet ketch with a large, shaded cockpit and lots of deckspace. Maximum of 6 passengers for whalewatch, sail, snorkel and sunset cruises. There is also a 36 feet racing sloop *Ranger* available for private and special charters. Ph 661 3448 for information and reservations.

Molokini Snorkel/Picnic Sail, ph 661 8600. Sail to the sealife-filled extinct volcanic crater Molokini aboard the *Coral Sea*, a glassbottom motor yacht. Six-hour picnic/snorkel cruise, including snorkelling gear, continental breakfast, buffet lunch and open bar.

SOUTH MAUI

Pacific Whale Foundation, Maalaea Harbour, slip no. 52. The 53 feet research vessel *Whale I* has 2.5 hour cruises departing daily at

7.30 and 10.30am, 1.30 and 4.15pm. All the profits from these cruises go toward marine research. If there are no whales at the time of the cruise, passengers receive a coupon for another trip, ph 879 8811.

Blue Water Rafting, Kihei boat launch, have large inflatable boats for parties of 6 to Molokini Crater — $29. They also have a deluxe tour which snorkels in different areas within the crater — ph 879-RAFT.

Steve's Diving Adventures, 1993 S. Khiei Road (in the Island Surf Building). Scuba dive in the volcanic crater of Molokini under the direction of 20-year dive veteran Frank Cushing. Beach, boat and night dives can also be arranged, ph 879 0055.

TOURS

Air

Alexair Air have tours over the valleys and mountains of Maui in their Hughes 500 Jet helicopter, with individual two-way headsets between pilot and passenger, ph 871 0792.

Cardinal Helicopters, Kahului heliport, have specially mounted camcorders to record your flight on VHS video, including the narration, ph 661 0092.

Hawaii Helicopters, Kahului Airport (commuter terminal), ph 877 3900, have daily flightseeing tours, personally narrated. Their jet helicopters are also air-conditioned.

Maui Helicopters, Maui Inter-Continental Hotel, Wailea, ph 879 1601 or 877 4333. New jet choppers fly several different tours.

Roberts Hawaii, Kaonowai Street, Kahului, ph 871 6226, advertise they have the best way to get a close-up view of the world's most active volcano, Kilauea.

South Sea Helicopters, ph 871 8844, have a variety of tours starting at $80 per person.

Sunshine Helicopters, ph 661 3047. Their pilot, Ross Scott, flies his 4-passenger Bell 206B Jet Ranger on custom-made trips from $49 per person.

Bicycle

Cruiser Bob's Legendary Haleakala Downhill is one of Maui's best known adventures. There are daily sunrise and picnic rides on custom-built bikes with mega-brakes. Rental bikes are also available. Call in at 505 Front Street, Lahaina, or ph 667 7717.

Maui Mountain Cruisers also bike down the slopes of Haleakala on their competitively priced tours. They have a sunrise cruise which includes continental breakfast at the summit, and a champagne brunch at Koho's Restaurant. The midday cruise includes a fresh pineapple/pastries breakfast at the Sunrise Country Market and a delicious lunch. They use individually-adjusted mountain cruiser bikes with ultrabrakes, safety apparel and transportation, ph 572 0195.

Car

If you intend to drive the 84km (52 miles) Highway 36 to Hana, a good tip is to get in touch with Hana Cassette Guides, ph 572 0550. They are located at the Shell Service Station on Route 380, just before Highway 36, Kahalui. The package includes a cassette player, photo album to help you identify Maui's exotic flowers, a comprehensive map and other useful information.

SPORT AND RECREATION

Golf

Maui Parbusters Golf Schools, Pukalani Country Club and Range, have lessons and clinics. Open 7am–9pm, ph 572 8062 — Green fees — 18 holes — $40.

Waiehu Municipal Golf Course, Waiehu, ph 244 5433 — Green fees — 18 holes — $15 (weekdays), $20 (weekends).

Kapalua Golf Course, Kapalua, ph 669 8044 — Green fees — 18 holes — guest $55, non-guest $85.

Royal Kaanapali Golf Course, Kaanapali, ph 661 3691 — Green fees — 18 holes — $74 daily.

Horseriding

Rainbow Ranch, at mile marker no. 29 in Napili, 10 minutes north of Kaanapali, ph 669 4991. Pony Express Tours, Makawao, ph 667 2202. Thompson Ranch Riding Stables, Kula, ph 878 1910.

MOLOKAI

Molokai is the fifth largest island of the Hawaiian group, with an area of 676km^2 (261 sq miles), and was formed by two major volcanic domes thousands of years ago.

It is now called the Friendly Isle, but was known in ancient times as the Lonely Isle because the powers of its priests were feared throughout the islands. Warring chiefs ignored Molokai, while persecuted natives sought refuge there.

King Kamehameha I took over the island in 1795 when he was on his way to conquer Oahu.

During the next century, leprosy (Hansen's Disease) struck the islands and the Kalaupapa Peninsula became the place of exile for the disease's victims. From 1866, lepers were forced to leave their families and live on this shore. The settlement was made famous by Father Damien, a Belgian priest who arrived in Kalaupapa in 1873 to spend a few weeks among the lepers. He stayed until his death, from the disease, in 1889.

Today Molokai is just the place to 'get away from it all'. It is closest to the spirit of Old Hawaii — it has no traffic lights, and a local newspaper that comes out every two weeks. Fences are often made from fallen trees to keep grazing cattle and horses off the roads, but remember that the occasional deer, pheasant or family of quail may claim right of way.

HOW TO GET THERE

Molokai is 42km (26 miles) east of Oahu — approximately 20 minutes by air from Honolulu to Molokai Airport.

Hawaiian Air offers daily flights to Molokai, and there are a number of scheduled commuter and other air taxi services providing frequent flights.

TOURIST INFORMATION

The Hawaii Visitors' Bureau does not have an office on Molokai.

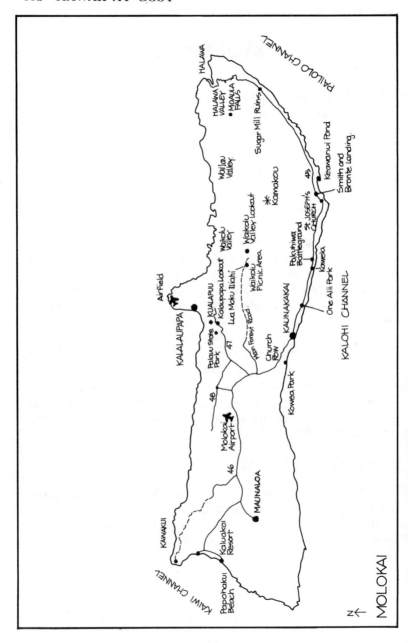

ACCOMMODATION

There is not a great deal of accommodation on Molokai, but here we have listed a few examples, with prices per person for a double room, per night. These prices should be used as a guide only.

Kaluakokoi Hotel and Golf Club, P.O. Box 1977, Maunaloa, ph 552 2555 — on Kepuhi Beach — $79–115; Paniolo Hale, P.O. Box 146, Maunaloa, ph 552 2731 — on Kepuhi Beach — apartments — $75–115; Ke Nani Kai, P.O. Box 126, ph 552 2761 — apartments — on oceanfront — $75–105; Hotel Molokai, P.O. Box 546, Kaunakakai, ph 553 5347 — cottage — on oceanfront — $55–105; Molokai Shores, Star Route, Kaunakakai, ph 553 5954 — apartments — on beach — $68–77; Pau Hana Inn, P.O. Box 860, Kaunakakai, ph 553 5342 — cottage — on oceanfront — $39–79.

LOCAL TRANSPORT

The choice here is between walking and hitching, or driving. Actually hitchhiking is illegal, but the police don't enforce this much. There are a few car rental companies:

Avis Rent A Car, Hoolehua Airport, Kaunakakai, ph 567 6814;
Tropical Rent-A-Car, Molokai Airport, Kaunakakai, ph 567 6118;
Molokai Island U-Drive, ph 567 6156.
There are no 4WD rental agencies on the island.

Distance and Driving Times
From Molokai Airport to:
Kaunakakai — 13km (8 miles) — 10 minutes.
Palaau Park — 14km (9 miles) — 15 minutes.
Kamalo — 23km (14 miles) — 30 minutes.
Halawa Valley — 58km (36 miles) — 2 hours.
Kepuhi Beach — 24km (15 miles) — 25 minutes.

EATING OUT

Molokai is not a gourmet's paradise, but you won't starve. Along Ala Malama Street in Kaunakakai, there are several budget restaurants. And at the other end of the scale, the Sheraton Hotel has the Ohia Lodge, ph 552 2555, which is everything you expect from a Sheraton restaurant, including the prices. Open breakfast, lunch and dinner. The Hotel also has a snack bar which serves sandwiches, etc.

Hop Inn, Ala Malama Street, ph 553 5465, is open daily 11am–9pm and has budget Chinese food.

Kanemitsu's Bakery, Ala Malama Street, ph 553 5855, is great for an economical but tasty breakfast.

Mid-Nite Inn, Ala Malama Street, ph 553 5302, open daily for breakfast, lunch and dinner, is also budget priced.

In the Hotel Molokai, 3km east of Kaunakakai, is the Holoholo Dining Room, ph 553 5347, which has a steak/seafood menu — expensive.

The Pau Hana Inn, ph 553 5342, has moderately priced lunch and dinner menus, and a very Hawaiian atmosphere.

Oviedo's Lunch Counter, ph 553 5014 and Rabang's Restaurant, ph 553 5878, are both on Ala Malama Street, and specialise in Filipino food at very reasonable prices.

ENTERTAINMENT

Again there is not much doing in the way of nightlife. The Sheraton's Ohia Lounge, ph 552 2555, has live music each night.

The Pau Hana Inn, ph 553 5342, has live entertainment, and is very popular with the local people.

Holoholo Dining Room, ph 553 5347, has an Hawaiian band Thurs–Sun.

SHOPPING

Molokai is paradise for those poor men who have been dragged into every shop since they left home by their better-half, and who have to carry the ever-increasing luggage. The shopping on the island is zilch with a capital Z.

SIGHTSEEING

KAUNAKAKAI AND SOUTH SHORE
Kaunakakai Town
The town is much the same as it was in the 1920s, and is the hub of the island — all roads lead to Kaunakakai. At the end of the town,

barges load and unload their cargoes at the wharf of the deep-water harbour, alongside local fishing boats.

Nearby are the remains of the home of King Kamehameha V, and down the street is the extensive Kapuaiwa Coconut Grove planted by the king, bordering a beach park. The beach offers safe swimming, but not much in the way of surfing.

West of the town there is a row of small, quaint churches of nearly every denomination.

On Hotel Lane is the Guze Ji Soto Mission (1927), the only Buddhist mission on Molokai. It is open only for services.

KAUNAKAKAI TO HALAWA

One Alii Park
The park is just east of Kaunakakai and is a pleasant spot for a picnic, with views of Lanai. There are rest-rooms, a pavilion, drinking water and camping facilities. An offshore reef makes the water very shallow and protected.

Kawela
Several kilometres from Kaunakakai there is a signposted route to Kawela and the nearby Pakuhiwa Battleground. It was from here that Kahemahema I launched an armada of canoes supposedly 4 miles wide.

Kamakou
The volcanic dome is the highest point on Molokai — 1,515m (4,970 ft). This is the site of the Nature Conservancy's 1,094ha (2,700 acres) Kamakou Preserve with its rare plants and birds.

St Joseph's Church
Built in 1876 by Father Damien, the church was restored in 1971, but is no longer used for services.

Smith and Bronte Landing
On the ocean side, a monument and plaque have been erected where Ernest Smith and Emory Bronte safely crashlanded their plane on June 14, 1927. The landing ended the first civilian trans-Pacific flight of 25 hours and 2 minutes.

Keawenui and Ualapue Fishponds
These two fishponds have been made a part of a National Historic
Landmark. Keawenui Pond covers 22ha (54.5 acres) and is sur-
rounded by a 610m (2,000 ft) wall.

The ancient people depended on fish for their very existence,
and fishing was also enjoyed as a sport by royalty and commoner
alike.

Fish were caught with nets, hooks and lines, spears, traps,
poisons as well as by hand. They were also captured in hundreds of
fishponds that at one time dotted the coastlines of all the islands.
The ponds belonged exclusively to the kings and chiefs. The
commoners, though they built, maintained and stocked the ponds,
could fish the sea only beyond the ponds.

They were constructed by building stone walls in shallow
offshore areas and at the mouth of natural inlets. A type of sluice
gate (makaha) was used to allow small fish to enter, and stop large
fish from leaving. The ponds were usually no deeper than three or
four feet, allowing sunlight to shine through the water and
encourage the growth of foods for the fish to feed upon.

The ruins of fishponds can be found throughout the Hawaiian
Islands, but there are more on Molokai than the others. At one
time there were 58 along this island's coast.

Kaluaaha Church
The first missionary, Rev H.R. Hitchcock, built this first Christian
church on Molokai in 1844.

Our Lady of Sorrows Catholic Church
Built by Father Damien in 1874, this is the second Catholic church
to be built on the island. Next to the church is a pavilion
containing a life-sized statue of Father Damien which was carved
by a local resident, John Kadowaki.

Octopus Stone
Opposite Kupeke Fishpong, there is a stone, painted white, at the
edge of the highway where the road turns sharply inland. Legend
says that the stone is the remainder of a cave where a supernatural
octopus lived, and some believe that the stone still has special
powers.

Wailau Trail
The trail is on private property and is the only access to the largest of the north coast valleys, once a population centre of ancient Hawaii. The trail is very difficult.

Iliiliopae Heiau
Again, this heiau is on private property, but may be visited with permission. It is on the National Register of Historic Places, and is one of the largest heiaus in Hawaii, being 98m (320 ft) long and 37m (120 ft) wide. The heiau was a site of human sacrifice.

Puu Mano
The focus of many legends about the Shark God.

Wailua
Kamehemeha Nui was raised here solely on taro leaves so that fishbones could not choke him. His giant awa cup is found near the stream. A rock by the road is said to have had an ear that could hear an enemy approaching, and the taro patch is just off the road.

Moanui Sugar Mill
The ruins and the stock are all that remain of a sugar mill which operated between 1870 and 1900. It was built and managed by Eugene Bal.

Puu O Hoku Ranch
"Hill of the Stars" is lush green ranchland with a magnificent view of the seascape. A working ranch with plenty of cattle and horses.

Lanikaula Grove
Just beyond the ranch buildings, between the road and the sea, is a sacred grove of kukui trees which is the burial place of Lanikaula, a Molokai prophet. The grove is on private land, but can easily be seen from the road.

Halawa Valley
The road zigzags down the ridge into the valley. There is good swimming in the bay and the mouth of the stream which divides the area. There is also a hiking track of 4km to Moaula Falls, which takes about an hour, but can be difficult if there has been a lot of rain.

UPPER MOLOKAI FROM KAUNAKAKAI TO KALAUPAPA LOOKOUT

Sandalwood Pit

Approximately 14km (9 miles) along the Main Forest Road, which is strictly for 4WD or hiking, there is the Lua Moku Iliahi (Sandalwood Pit). The pit was dug the size of the hold of a ship, and the sandalwood placed inside. When it was full the wood was transferred to the harbour and loaded aboard a waiting ship.

Waikolu Valley

Along the Main Forest Road, just past the Sandalwood Pit is a lovely picnic area with views into the inaccessible valley which opens to the north side of the island.

Kualapuu (on route 48)

A former pineapple plantation town and the site of the world's largest rubber-lined reservoir.

Kauluwai

From here Oahu can be seen on a clear day. King Kamehameha I camped for a year in this area to train and condition his troops before attacking Oahu.

Kaiae

Now a residential area, Kaiae was the former dwelling place of chiefs. It was here that Rudolph W. Meyer, a German who married High Chieftainess Kalama, built a home in 1851.

Palaau Park

At the end of the road on route 47, is a wilderness of koa, paperback, ironwood and cypress trees. There is also a small arboretum with 40 species of trees labelled, and a camping ground with a pavilion and picnic area.

Kalaupapa Lookout

From the lookout there is a spectacular view of Kalaupapa, the wharf, churches, lighthouse, landing field, and crater, 488m (1600 ft) below.

Phallic Rock

About 180 (200 yards) through the woods is a 180cm (6 ft) high rock to which early Hawaiian women made offerings for fertility.

Kalaupapa

A visit to Kalaupapa is a definite must, but remember that children under 16 are not admitted. The leper colony still exists, but the few remaining inhabitants are free to come and go, as the disease has been controlled with sulphone drugs since 1946. The only reason the patients still stay is that they are elderly, and having lived most of their lives at the settlement, they have no where else to go.

It was in 1866 that the Hawaiian government commenced exiling lepers to this lonely spot. Kalaupapa was then a fishing village, so the lepers were sent to the old settlement at Kalawao on the eastern side of the peninsula. The boats they came in anchored off the coast, and the lepers were forced overboard and had to make their own way to the inhospitable land.

The terrible conditions continued until the arrival in 1873 of Joseph Damien de Veuster, Father Damien. Although he only intended to stay for a short time, the plight of the people changed his mind, and he stayed until his death from the disease in 1889. He built a simple wooden church, St Philomena's, in 1871, and in the nearby cemetery there is a monument to this martyr. He was originally buried here, but his remains were returned to Belgium in the 1930s. Services are still held in the church.

Now designated a National Historical Park, Kalaupapa can be reached by air (Princeville Airways, ph 567 6115), by mule (Molokai Mule Ride, ph 567 6088) or by foot (Damien Tour, ph 567 6171). The mule train trip takes 90 minutes to wind its way down the 610m (2,000 ft) trail from the Kalaupapa Lookout. Although it may look a bit dicey, it is actually a very safe trip, and many say the experience of a lifetime.

Pali Coastline

The highlights of this coastline are the world's highest sea cliffs, and waterfalls plunging thousands of metres into the ocean. Air sightseeing tours and boats from Kaunakakai are available.

WEST MOLOKAI FROM KAUNAKAKAI

Molokai Ranch. Wildlife Park

Here is an adventure of a different kind — an 'African' safari. The 324ha (800 acres) park is an animal preserve for rare and endangered hoofed animals, and the terrain and vegetation are similar to that of the plains of Kenya and Tanzania. Living in the wild are Barbary sheep, eland, Indian black buck, sable antelope, impala, oryx, ibex, greater kudu, giraffe, ostrich, rhea, sika and axis deer — more than 400 animals in all for you to 'shoot', with a camera of course.

Kaluakoi Resort
The Resort stretches 4km (2.5 miles) along Papohaku, Hawaii's largest white sand beach. The complex includes a luxury hotel and resort condominiums with approximately 500 units in one and two storey Polynesian-style buildings, an 18-hole championship golf course, tennis courts, a shopping arcade and first class restaurants.

Maunaloa
Formerly a Dole plantation town, Manualoa is now virtually a ghost town with quaint buildings, but there are some shops selling works by Molokai artists and craftsmen.

TOURS

Apart from the Kalaupapa tours already mentioned, Gray Line Molokai, ph 567 6177, and Roberts Hawaii, ph 552 2751, have general full-day and half-day tours which include the points of interest, such as the Halawa Valley, Kaunakakai and the Kalaupapa lookout. Prices, of course, depend on the length of the tour. The Nature Conservancy of Hawaii has tours of the rain forests and mountains of all the islands, so on this isle they have tours to Kamakou Preserve and Moomomi Dunes. Their address is 1116 Smith Street, Honolulu.

SPORT AND RECREATION

Golf
Ironwood Hills Golf Course, Kalae, ph 567 6121. Green fees — 9 holes — $5 daily.

   Kalua Koi Golf Course (Sheraton-Molokai), ph 552 2739. Green fees — 18 holes — guest $40, non-guest $55.

Horse Riding
Halawa Valley Horse Rides, ph 553 3214.

KAUAI

Kauai is the oldest of the Hawaiian chain, both geographically and historically. It is nearly circular in shape, and is arguably the most beautiful of the islands. It was on the Garden Isle that the movies *South Pacific* and *King Kong* were filmed, but even these did not do justice to the natural scenery of the island.

Kauai was the first of the islands to be visited by Captain Cook in 1778, and it was the last to be an independent kingdom. It was the only island not conquered by Kamehameha the Great in his battles to be the king of a united Hawaii. It was only by diplomacy that he arranged a treaty with King Kaumualii of Kauai.

The first successful sugar plantation was established here, and it is the only island where the fragrant mokihana berry grows. The island is very rich in folklore, and the islanders are very proud of their heritage and history. The legendary race of little people, the Menehune, were very active on Kauai. Believed to be about 61cm (2 ft) tall with ugly red faces and big eyes, they were nocturnal workers who in one night achieved the construction of the Alekoko fish pond at Niumalu, and the Menehune watercourse of Waimea Valley. There are some people today on Kauai who claim Menehune ancestry, and who say that the little people are still on the island, hiding in the dense forests.

Kauai is 153km (95 miles) north-west of Oahu, and has an area of 1,432km² (553 sq miles).

HOW TO GET THERE

Aloha Airlines, Hawaiian Air and Mid Pacific Air have frequent daily flights to Lihue Airport. There are also scheduled commuter and other air taxi services operating between the Islands.

Princeville Airways offers flights from Princeville Airport.

In addition, the island is served directly from mainland United States by a regular United Airlines service from Los Angeles and San Francisco.

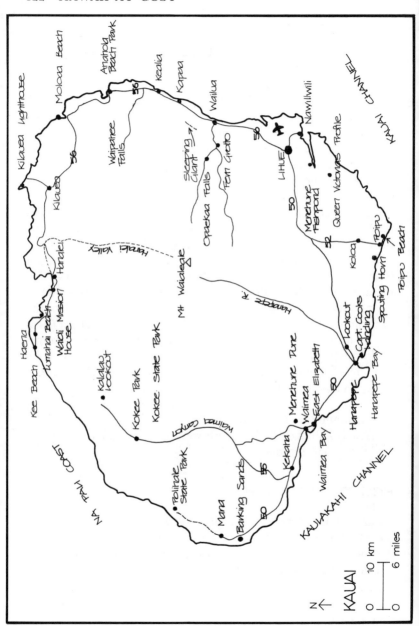

TOURIST INFORMATION

The Hawaii Visitor's Bureau have an office in the Lihue Plaza Building.

ACCOMMODATION

No shortages in this area on Kauai. The accommodation listed here is for a twin share room per person per night, and should be used as a guide only.

Lihue/Nawiliwili
Westin Kauai, Kalapaki Beach, Lihue, ph 245 5050 — on sandy beach — $185; Plantation Hale, 484 Kuhio Highway, Kapaa, ph 822 4941 — apartments — in coconut plantation — $95–105; Tip Top Motel, 3173 Akahi Street, Lihue — $28–34; Hale Pumehana, P.O. Box 1828, Lihue, ph 245 2106 — motel — $22; Ocean View Motel, 3445 Wilcox Road, Lihue, ph 245 6345 — $22.

Waipouli
Kaha Lani, 4460 Nehe Road, Lihu, ph 822 9331 — apartments on the beach — $109–165; Aston Kauai Resort, 3–5920 Kuhio Highway, Kapaa, ph 245 3931 — hotel on Wailua beach - - $89–139; Kauai Hilton, 4331 Kauai Beach Drive, Lihue, ph 245 1955 — on Waipouli beach — $125; Lac Nani, 410 Papaloa Road, Kapaa — apartments on beach — $130–170; Coco Palms Resort Hotel, P.O. Box 631, Lihue, ph 822 4921 — across road from Wailua Beach — $105–110; Kapaa Shore, 40–900 Kuhio Highway, Kapaa, ph 822 3055 — apartments on ocean front — $80–110; Sheraton Coconut Beach Hotel, Coconut Plantation, Kapaa, ph 822 3455 — on Waipouli beach — $105; Kauai Beachboy, 484 Kuhio Highway, Kapaa, ph 822 3441 — hotel on Waipouli beach — $78–88; Islander on the Beach, 4–484 Kuhio Highway, Kapaa, ph 822 7417 — hotel on the beach — $78–88; Kauai Sands Hotel, 420 Papaloa Road, Coconut Plantation, Wailua, ph 822 4951 — on Waipouli beach — $52–64; Kapaa Sands, 380 Papaloa Road, Kapaa, ph 822 4901 — apartments on ocean front — $59; Hotel Coral Reef, 1516 Kuhio Highway, Kapaa, ph 822 4481 — $32–52; Kay Barker's Bed & Breakfast, P.O. Box 740, Kapaa — Wailua area — $30–35.

Hanalei/Princeville

Sheraton Princeville Hotel, P.O. Box 3069, Princeville, ph 826 9644 — ocean front — $195–295; Steeb Home, P.O. Box 1109, Hanalei, ph 826 9833 — Princeville on golf course — $185–225; Mauna Makai, P.O. Box 1109, Hanalei, ph 826 9833 — hotel — $165; Pu'u Po'a, P.O. Box 1109, Hanalei, ph 826 9833 — apartments in Princeville — $125–165; Ka'eo Kai, P.O. Box 1109, Hanalei, ph 826 9833 — Princeville — $125–145; Hale Makai Beach Cottages, P.O. Box 1109, Hanalei, ph 826 9833 — ocean front — $125–135; Alii Kaii, P.O. Box 1109, Hanalei, ph 826 9833 — apartments ocean front at Princeville — $110–130; Pumana, P.O. Box 1109, Hanalei, ph 826 9833 — apartments 0.5km from Anini Beach — $85–125; Paliuli Cottages, P.O. Box 351, Hanalei — near Hanalei Beach — $100–120; Mauna Kai, Hanalei, ph 826 9833 — apartments at Anini Beach — $85–110; Paniolo, P.O. Box 1109, Hanalei, ph 827 9833 — apartments in Princeville — $80–110; Hale Moi, P.O. Box 1109, Hanalei, ph 826 9833 — apartments in Princeville — $80–110; Hanalei Colony Resort, P.O. Box 206, Hanalei, ph 826 6235 — apartments on Haena beach — $100–105; Sea Lodge, P.O. Box 1109, Hanalei, ph 826 9833 — apartments on Princeville ocean front — $85–105; Sandpiper Village, P.O. Box 3485, Hanalei, ph 826 9613 — apartments 1km from Hanalei Bay — $70–100; Waimea Plantation Cottages, P.O. Box 367, Waimea, ph 338 1625 — $65–100; Hanalei Bay Resort, P.O. Box 1109, Hanalei, ph 826 9833 — hotel on sand beach — $80–90.

Poipu/Kokee

Kiahuna Beachside, P.O. Box 369, Koloa, ph 742 7262 — apartments on beach — $100–350; Whalers Cove, 2640 Puuholo Road, Koloa, ph 742 7572 — apartments — $250; Poipu Kai, RR1 Box 173, Koloa, ph 742 6464 — apartments at Poipu — $120–160; Aston Poipu at Makahuena, 1661 Pe'e Road, Koloa, ph 742 9555 — apartments — $99–160; Lawai Beach Resort, 5017 Lawai Road, Koloa, ph 742 9581 — apartments across from beach — $90–150; Sheraton Kauai Hotel, 2440 Hoonani Road, Koloa, ph 742 1661 — on beach — $140; Stouffer's Waiohai Beach Resort, 2249 Poipu Road, Koloa, ph 742 9511 — hotel on beach — $135; Kiahuna Plantation, RR1 P.O. Box 73, Koloa, ph 742 6411 — apartments on beach — $120–130; Poipu Shores Resort, 1775 Pe'e Road, Koloa, ph 742 7700 — $100–125; Nih Kai Villas, 1870 Hoone Road, RR 1, Koloa, ph 742 6458 — apartments in Poipu - $112; Poipu Bed and Breakfast Inn, 2720 Hoonani Road, Koloa, ph 742 1146 — $65–100; Waimea Plantation Cottages, P.O. Box 367, Waimea, ph 338 1625 — $65–100. Stouffer's Poipu Beach Resort, 2251 Poipu Road, Koloa, ph 742 1681 — on beach — $85; Sunset Kahili, 1763 Poe Road, Koloa, ph 742 1691 — on ocean front — $73–80; Prince Kuhio Rentals, P.O. Box 1060, Koloa, ph 742 1409 — apartments — $44–54; Garden Isle Cottages, 2666 Puuholo Road, Koloa, ph 742 6717 — apartment/cottages on ocean front — $43–45; Kokee Lodge, P.O. Box 819, Waimea, ph 335 6061 — cabins — $35–45; Poipu Executive Beach Rentals, P.O. Box 99, Koloa, ph 742 1243 — apartments — $44.

LOCAL TRANSPORT

There is no local bus service, so renting a car is the only way to go. Here are a few names and addresses:

Avis Rent A Car, P.O. Box 786, Lihue, ph 245 3512, and Princeville Airport, ph 826 9773.

Budget Rent A Car, Lihue Airport, ph 245 9031.

Dollar Rent-a-Car Systems of Hawaii, Lihue Airport, ph 245 3653.

Hertz Rent A Car, Lihue Airport, ph 245 3356.

National Car Rental, Lihue Airport, ph 245 5637.

Roberts Hawaii, Lihue Airport, ph 245 9558.

Trac Systems, Inc., 4031 Kalau Street, Lihue, ph 245 4219.

Tropical Rent-A-Car, 3156 Oihana Street, Lihue, ph 245 6988.

United Car Rental Systems, Box 173-A Lihue, ph 245 8894.

Most of the roads on Kauai are accessible by car, but if you would still like to get around in a jeep, there's Rent-A-Jeep, 3137A Kuhio Highway, Lihue, ph 245 9622.

Distance and Driving Times
From Lihue to:

Poipu — 23km (14 miles) — 40 minutes.

Waimea — 40km (25 miles) — 1 hour.

Kekaha — 47km (29 miles) — 1 hour 5 minutes.

Waimea Canyon — 64km (40 miles) — 2 hours.

Kalalau Lookout — 80km (50 miles) — 2 hours 10 minutes.
Wailua River — 11km (7 miles) — 20 minutes.
Hanalei — 56km (35 miles) — 1 hour 15 minutes.
Haena — 66km (41 miles) — 1 hour 30 minutes.

EATING OUT

Most of the hotels have excellent dining rooms and restaurants, but if you occasionally feel like something different, here are a few names and addresses.

Lihue Area
J.J.'s Broiler, 2971 Haleko Road, ph 245 3841 — steaks and salad — moderate.

The Eggbert's, 4483 Rice Street, ph 245 6325 — omelettes, vegetarian — moderate.

Casa Italiana, 2989 Haleko Road, ph 245 9586 — good Italian — moderate.

Barbeque Inn, 2982 Kress Street, ph 245 2921 — Asian and American — moderate.

Tip Top Cafe and Bakery, 3173 Akahi Street, ph 245 2333 — breakfast, lunch and dinner — budget.

Harbour Village, opposite the Westin Kauai, has several small restaurants.

Ma' Family, 4277 Halenani Street, ph 245 312 — open for breakfast and lunch — budget.

Hamura Saimin, 2956 Kress Street, ph 245 3271 — Oriental, open lunch and dinner — budget.

Restaurant Kiibo, 2991 Umi Street, ph 245 2650 — Japanese — moderate.

Poipu Area
Plantation Gardens Restaurant, opposite the Sheraton, ph 742 1695 — Continental, dinner only — expensive.

Keoki's Paradise, Kiahuna Shopping Village, ph 742 7534 — steaks and seafood, dinner only — moderate.

Koloa Broiler, 5412 Koloa Road, ph 742 9122 — cook your own — moderate.

Brennecke's Seaside Bar and Grill, Hoona Road, 742 7588 — seafood — moderate.

Waimea Area

Linda's, Hanapepe Road, ph 335 5152 — open breakfast and lunch — budget.

Traveler's Den II, Kekaha Road, Kekaha, ph 337 9922 — open breakfast and lunch — budget.

Green Garden Restaurant, Route 50, Hanapepe, ph 335 5422 — breakfast, lunch and dinner, extensive menu — moderate.

Wrangler's Restaurant, Route 50, Waimea, ph 338 1218 — lunch and dinner, American — moderate.

Wailua Area

Duane's Ono Burger, Route 56, Anahola, ph 822 9181 — American — budget.

J.J.'s Broiler Room, in the Market Place of the Coconut Plantation, Route 56, Wailua — similar, but larger, than the broiler room in Lihue -- moderate.

Kapaa Fish & Chowder House, 1639 Kuhio Highway, Kapaa, ph 822 7488 — open lunch and dinner — moderate.

Seashell Restaurant, Kuhio Highway, Wailua, ph 822 3632 — seafood and steaks — expensive.

Hanalei Area

Hanalei Shell House, ph 826 9301 — open breakfast, lunch and dinner, homemade type food — moderate.

Charo's, Route 56, 8km north of Hanalei, ph 826 6422 — open lunch and dinner, excellent menu -- expensive.

Tahiti Nui Restaurant, ph 826 6277 — Hawaiian cuisine with a luau Mon, Wed and Fri — expensive.

Hanalei Dolphin Restaurant, beside the Hanalei River, ph 826 6113 — open 6–10pm, seafood and steaks — expensive.

ENTERTAINMENT

Kauai could never be called the nightlife capital of anywhere, but there is usually somethihg happening in the large hotels, and there are a few local lounges you could try.

Lihue Area

Lihua Cafe Lounge, 2978 Umi Street, ph 245 671; Park Place, Harbour Village Shopping Centre, ph 245 5775; Club Jetty, Nawiliwili, ph 245 4970.

Poipu Area
Brennecke's Seaside Bar & Grill, Honna Road, ph 742 7588; Waiohai Hotel, Poipu Beach, ph 742 9511; Mahina Lounge, Poipu Beach Hotel, ph 742 1681.

Wailua Area
Gilligans, 4331 Kauai Beach Drive (Hilton), ph 245 1955; Boogie Palace, Kauai Beach Boy Hotel, ph 822 3441; Jolly Roger, Market Place in Coconut Plantation, ph 822 3451; Lagoon Cocktail Terrace, Coco Palms Hotel, ph 822 4921; Seashell Restaurant, Route 56, Wailua, ph 822 3632.

Hanalei Area
Tortilla Flats Restaurant and Cantina, Princeville Centre, ph 826 7255; Tahiti Nui Restaurant, Hanalei, ph 826 6277; Lime Tree Lounge, Sheraton Princeville, ph 826 9644.

SHOPPING

Kukui Grove Center, Route 50, 1km from Lihue, is the island's largest shopping centre with department stores, bookshops and specialty stores.

Kilohana, Route 50 about 2km west of Lihue, is set in an old plantation house in 14ha (35 acres) of well-kept grounds. If you can't see anything you fancy to buy, at least the surroundings are beautiful.

Kapaia Stitchery, Route 56, Kapaia, ph 245 2281, has local handicrafts, including aloha shirts, Hawaiian quilting kits and dresses and patchwork quilts.

Old Koloa Town, on Koloa Road on the way to Poipu, has several small shops.

The Spouting Horn in the car park at the blowhole, is a fascinating place. Local merchants set up stalls and sell their wares. If you are interested in local jewellery, here you can watch it being made, then barter for it.

Kiahuna Shopping Village on Poipu Road has a range of up-market shops.

Bougainvilla, 3900 Hanapepe Road, Hanapepe, ph 3355 3582, has clothing and jewellery, as well as hand-made teddy bears. Upstairs is the James Hoyle Gallery, with displays of works of famous Hawaiian artists.

The Art Hut, Hanapepe Road, Hanapepe, ph 245 9143, has oil paintings by artist Ales Sedlacek.

The Market Place at Coconut Plantation, Route 56, Wailua, is the best shopping centre on Kauai. The little wooden stores are designed as plantation houses, and you will be able to find anything you are looking for.

The Coco Palms Hotel has several rather expensive shops selling handicrafts. Incidentally this is where *Blue Hawaii*, with Elvis Presley, was filmed.

Rehabilitation Unlimited of Kauai, 4531 Kuamoo Road, ph 822 4975, has on offer bamboo and coconut wares made by local disabled folk.

Princeville Center, off Route 56, is a good place for window-shopping unless you have a large budget.

Kong Lung Co, Kilauea, ph 828 1822, stocks Asian and Pacific treasures, and is worth a visit.

The Native Hawaiian Trading and Cultural Center, in Hanalei, has many small shops selling the usual Hawaiian objects, and a small Hawaiian artifacts museum. Next door is a modern shopping mall, Ching Young Village.

SIGHTSEEING

Lihue
The colourful town of Lihue, Kauai's commercial centre, is the starting point for a tour of either half of the Garden Isle.

Sugar cane was first planted here around 1835, making it one of the oldest plantation towns in the Islands. The town houses the state and county offices, and has a regional library and convention centre. Other places of interest include:

The Kauai Museum, ph 245 6931, presents a factual history of the Garden Isle, using artifacts and photographs.

Follow Rice Street to Nawiliwili, turn on to Route 58, then on to Niumalu Road, then Hulemalu Road, and you will come to the Menehune Fish Pond The pond is spread across a valley floor, and is believed by some to have been built in one night by the Menehunes.

The Grove Farm Homestead, just south of Lihue, was founded in 1864 by George Wilcox, and is now a museum complex that includes the old family plantation home, wash house, tea house, guest cottage, and other amenities. The homestead is typical of the old Hawaiian plantation experience and tradition.

SOUTH SHORE AREA

Queen Victoria's Profile

Along Route 50 on the left hand side when you are heading for Poipu, there is a Hawaii Visitors' Bureau sign pointing out the profile of Queen Victoria carved in the Hoary Head Range. You have to use your imagination for these sorts of things.

Koloa

The first sugar plantation in Hawaii was started here in 1835, but the town is rather tumbledown now.

Poipu Beach

The park here has picnic facilities, rest rooms, showers, volleyball, playground, lifeguards, and excellent swimming. The entire area around here has some of the best diving spots on the island.

Spouting Horn

At high tide the waves force water through lava tubes, and out a hole in the rocks to form a really spectacular fountain of spray and foam. Not your ordinary blowhole.

Hanapepe

An old village complete with wooden sidewalks and weather-beaten houses and shops. There was a bit of trouble here in the sugar strike of 1924, with sixteen workers being killed, and the town still retains the same spirit of independence. It's worth a detour to have a look-see.

From the Hanapepe Valley Lookout there is good view of native flora set in a gorge surrounded by eroded cliffs.

Fort Elizabeth

An old Russian fort built by an employee of the Russian Fur Company of Alaska in 1817, who had high hopes of seizing Kauai for the Czar. The fort was near the mouth of the Waimea River, but all that remains of the Russian dream are a few rocky ruins.

Captain Cook's Landing

I wonder if anyone has ever counted how many monuments to Cook's landings there are in the Pacific region. Anyway, here's another. This commemorates the first place he landed in Hawaii in January 1778. Just follow the sign posts to the lava monolith. Waimea Bay was for many years a favourite provisioning port with Pacific traders and whalers.

Menehune Ditch
Only small portions remain of what was once a great water course. Archeologists say it was built before Hawaiians came, possibly by the Menehune, but no claims are made that it would built in one night. It's just outside Waimea, on Menehune Road.

Barking Sands
On Route 50, the 18m (60 ft) sand dunes are supposed to make a barking sound when ground underfoot. Personally I doubt it, but give it a go, you won't be the only person trying to make the sand bark. The beach is on a military reservation, so access is limited. Ph 335 4346 or 335 4356 to make sure you can enter.

Mana
A dilapidated town on the way to Polihale State Park, from where there is an excellent view of Niihau, the westernmost inhabited island of Hawaii. Niihau is privately-owned and several hundred natives live a life similar to that of 19th century Hawaii. Unfortunately, it is off limits to visitors.

Waimea Canyon
The 1,097m (3,600 ft) deep canyon is reached by taking Route 55 from Waimea, with fantastic views along the way.

Kokee Park
Adjacent to Waimea Canyon, Kokee Park (ph 335 5871) has picnic grounds, cabins and a wide variety of outdoor activities including hunting, trout fishing and hiking. The NASA Kokee Tracking Station is nearby.

Kalakau Lookout
Once peacocks preened their plumage in this tropic Eden, and natives cultivated terraces of taro. No one lives here now, but it is arguably one of the most beautiful views on earth.

NORTH SHORE AREA

Ke'e Beach
At the beginning (or end) of Route 56, where the Kalalau trail to the Na Pali Cliffs begins, is the reef-shrouded Ke'e Beach.

Wet and Dry Caves of Haena
Geologists say that the Maniniholo Dry Cave is a lava tube, but the natives 'know' it was built by the Menehunes. The Waikapalae and Waikanaloa Wet Caves nearby are also 'known' to be the creation of Pele, the fire goddess, who was looking for fire, but found water.

Lumahai Beach
Near the 33-mile marker on Route 56, a path leads to the partly reef-protected beach. Probably best known as the Nurse's Beach in the movie *South Pacific*, the swimming is generally pretty good, but still take care. Fishing is pretty good here, too.

Waioli Mission House
Visitors are most welcome at this quaint home built in 1834, and restored by the descendants of the first missionaries, ph 245 3202.

Hanalei Valley
Another name for Hanalei is Hanohano, meaning 'glorious', and that just about sums up the view gained from the Hanalei Valley Lookout on Route 56. The lower 365ha (900 acres) comprise a national wildlife refuge under the auspices of the US Fish and Wildlife Service to protect Hawaii's four endangered water birds — Hawaiian Stilt, Hawaiian Coot, Hawaiian Gallinule and Hawaiian Duck (or Koloa).

In, and near, the town of Hanalei there are incredible mountain views, tumbledown buildings and crescent beaches — altogether glorious.

Kilauea Lighthouse
Situated on the northernmost point of the principal islands of Hawaii, the lighthouse is the first beacon seen by sailors venturing east from Asia, and has the world's largest clamshell lens. It is open to visitors Sun–Fri, noon–4pm, and while there look closely at the nearby cliffs — you might be lucky enough to see albatross nesting.

Moloaa Beach
A secluded beach divided into two by a stream. It has good fishing and skin diving. Swim with care. It's on a side road off Route 56.

Anahola Beach
The park has a picnic area, rest rooms, showers and is less than 2km from the town of Anahola. There is a very strong current here, so swimmers should be careful. The fishing is good.

Kealia Beach
There are no picnic areas, rest rooms or showers, just a great beach opposite the 'one-horse' town of Kealia. The swimming is good (again with caution) and people fish here for ulua, papio and threadfin.

Kapaa Beach
A pretty little beach with the normal facilities, not far off Route 56 and Kapaa town. The swimming and fishing are okay.

The Sleeping Giant
The outline of a mountain ridge shows a striking resemblance to a reclining giant. It is supposed to be Puni, a friend of the Menehune.

Opaekaa Falls
Opaekaa means 'rolling shrimp' and dates from the days when swarms of shrimp were seen rolling in turbulent waters at the base of the falls. The scenery near the falls is worth a visit.

Royal Birth Stones, Wailua
On Route 580 the Visitors' Bureau has sign posts to the Holo'Holo'Ku Heiau, a very old temple and place of refuge and sacrifice, and to Pohaku Ho'Ohanau a sacred place in Hawaiian history. The women of Hawaiian nobility always tried to reach these sacred stones in time to give birth, to ensure the royal status of their children. Nearby are the remains of the king's house and the Bell Stone, which signalled the birth of a royal infant. This ancient noble place has been restored by the Bishop Museum and the Kauai Historical Society.

Smith's Tropical Paradise
A 9ha (23 acres) park with gardens, lagoons, exotic birds and a unique narrated train ride which wanders through a rain forest, a

Polynesian village, a Japanese island, a Filipino village and other interesting areas. Kauai's ethnic heritage is reflected nightly in a 75 minute musical production in the lagoon theatre.

Fern Grotto
Reached by ferry from the Wailua Marina, the grotto is a cave framed by ferns with a waterfall cascading to the rocks below. It's a popular place for wedding ceremonies.

Kamokila Hawaiian Village
Above the bend of the Wailua River, where war canoes of the King of Kauai, Kamualii, once assembled, lie the ruins of an old Hawaiian village. The village is open for visitors, and has daily craft demonstrations.

TOURS

Air
There are many flightseeing tours on offer. For example, Papillon Helicopters, Princeville Airport, ph 826 6591, have tours of the entire island for $115 per person, and a tour into Waialeale Crater, with breakfast and lunch included, for $225. There are several other companies with similar tours, and here we have a few names and addresses.

Lihue Area
Garden Island Helicopters, P.O. Box 3101, Lihue, ph 245 8588; South Sea Helicopter, Lihue Airport, ph 245 7781; Kauai Helicopters, Lihue Airport, ph 245 7403; Ohana Helicopters, 3222 Kuhio Highway, Lihue, ph 245 3996; Kenai Helicopter Tours, Lihue Airport, ph 245 8591; Menehune Helicopters Tours, 3222 Kuhio Highway, Lihue, ph 245 7705.

South Shore Area
Bruce Needham Helicopters, Hanapepe, ph 335 5009

North Shore Area
Blue Sky Aviation (Cessna), P.O. Box 724, Kilauea, ph 828 1344; Princeville Airways, Princeville Airport.

Land

Robert's Hawaii, P.O. Box 3389, Lihue, ph 245 9109, have an 8-hour guided tour to Waimea Canyon by bus for $28.85 per person.

Kauai Mountain Tours, P.O. Box 3069, Lihue, ph 245 7224, have 7-hour off-road tours of the Na Pali-Kona Forest Reserve, lunch included for $70 per person.

Gray Line, Lihue Airport, Lihue, ph 834 1033, have a Waimea Canyon/Wailua River trip for $25 plus $7 for the river boat.

Water

Captain Zodiac Raft Expeditions, P.O. Box 456, Hanalei, ph 826 9371, have tours along the Na Pali Coast, except in heavy surf. The cost is $90 for a full day, and $55 for a half day.

Na Pali-Kauai Boat Charters, P.O. Box 3224, Princeville, ph 826 7254, have seasonal whale-watching tours, and a day-long snorkelling trip for $85.

Smith's Motor Boat Service, 174 Wailua Road, Kapaa, ph 822 4111, have tours up the Wailua River to Fern Grotto for $8. If you decide to go Hawaiian and have your wedding there, they will take care of the lot for $250.

Other names and addresses: Lady Ann Cruises, P.O. Box 3422, Lihue, ph 245 8538; Pacific Adventure Cruises, 51–5144 Kuhio Highway, Hanalei, ph 826 9999; Fantasy Island Boat Tours, 2100 Haone Road, Koloa, Poipou Beach, ph 742 6636.

SPORT AND RECREATION

Golf

Wailua Municipal Golf Course, 4396 Rice Street, Lihue, ph 245 8092. Green fees — 18 holes — $10 weekdays, $11 weekends.

The Kiahuna Golf Club, RR1 Box 78, Koloa, ph 742 9595. Green fees — 18 holes — $50.

Kukuiolono Park and Golf Course, Kalaheo, ph 332 9151. Green fees — 9 holes — $5 daily.

Princeville Makai Golf Course, P.O. Box 3040, Princeville, ph 826 3580. Green fees — 9 holes — $27–34 guests, $44–50 non-guests.

Horse Riding
Po'oku Stables, P.O. Box 888, Hanalei, ph 826 6777 — Princeville area — valley rides $17; beach rides $35; waterfall rides (3-hour including lunch) $55.

High Gates Ranch, 6280 Olohena Road, Kapaa, ph 922 3182 — adults $18 per hour, children $9 per hour.

Snorkelling/Diving
Aquatics Kauai, 733 Kuhio Highway, Waipouli, ph 822 9422, offer half-day snorkelling trip for $45; half-day scuba instruction, $65, night dives $60.

Ocean Odyssey, P.O. Box 807, Kapaa, ph 822 9680, have dive and snorkel tours from $25.

Fathom Five Divers, P.O. Box 907, Koloa, ph 72 6991, is a dive shop with scuba instruction and daily trips. Beginner's dive, including gear hire is $60.

Sea Sage, 4–1378 Kuhio Highway, Kapaa, ph 822 3841, offer a 2-tank dive including gear for $75.

Na Pali Kai Tours, 1388 Kuhio Highway, Kapaa, ph 822 3553, have snorkelling trips at very competitive prices.

Freshwater Fishing
The rainbow trout season opens on the first Saturday in August for 16 days, after that fishing is permitted only on weekends and holidays until the end of September. Other freshwater fish may be caught daily all year round. A freshwater fishing licence is required and can be obtained from the Department of Land and Natural Resources, P.O. Box 1671, Lihue, ph 245 4433. A 30-day licence for visitors is $3.75.

Bass Guides of Kauai, P.O. Box 3525, Lihue, ph 822 1405 — half-day trip, $90 for 1 person, $125 for 2.

Deep-sea Fishing
Naa Pali Kauai Boat Charters, P.O. Box 3224, Princeville, ph 826 7254, have exclusive and shared trips from $55 to $75 per person.

Sportsfishing Kauai, P.O. Box 1185 Koloa, ph 742 7013, have shared and exclusive 4, 6 and 8 hour trips with a price range of from $85 to $600.

Sea Breeze Sportsfishing Charters, P.O. Box 594, Kilauea, ph 828 1285, have shared trips on the north shore for $70 per person.

Tennis

Over 70 of the hotels and resorts have their own tennis courts, which are free for guests but cost about $10 per hour per person for non-guests. There are roughly 20 public courts, and you should contact the Visitors' Bureau or the Country Department of Parks and Recreation, ph 245 8821, for information on bookings.

Waimea Canyon, Kauai

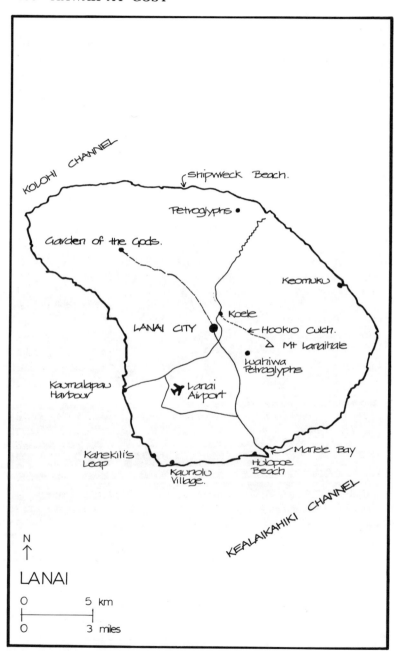

KOLOHI CHANNEL

Shipwreck Beach.

Petroglyphs

Garden of the Gods.

Keomuku

Koele

LANAI CITY

Hookio Gulch.

△ Mt Lanaihale

Luahiwa Petroglyphs

Kaumalapau Harbour

Lanai Airport

Kahekili's Leap

Kaunolu Village.

Manele Bay

Hulopoe Beach

KEALAIKAHIKI CHANNEL

N

LANAI

0   5 km

0   3 miles

LANAI

Lanai, the Pineapple Isle, is 77km (48 miles) south-east of Ohau, 13km (8 miles) west of Maui, and 11km (7 miles) south of Molokai. The island has an area of 363km^2 (140 sq miles), being 29km (18 miles) long and 21km (13 miles) wide. It is, like all the other islands in the Hawaiian group, of volcanic origin.

The island was discovered by that intrepid Englishman, Captain James Cook, in 1779, but because of its reef-shrouded shores and dry, barren-looking landscape, nobody bothered to stay. The ancient Hawaiians had not been too keen on Lanai either, because they believed it was inhabited by evil spirits, until the Maui chief Kakaalaneo banished his errant son, Kaululaau, to the island because of his atrocious behaviour on Maui. Whilst on Lanai, the wild young man took a change for the better and drove out all the evil spirits. Lanai was then settled by Hawaiians and controlled by Maui chiefs.

The first missionaries, Dwight Baldwin and William Richards, arrived in 1835, and by the 1850s the Mormons had established a City of Joseph in central Lania. This venture only lasted about three years, because the drought and insect plagues convinced the missionaries this was no Eden.

Then in 1922, Jim Dole's Hawaiian Pineapple Company bought a major portion of the island from Harry and Frank Baldwin, descendants of the early missionary, for about $1.1m (proving there is more money in land than in missionary work).

Another man who changed the face of Lanai was George Munro, a New Zealand naturalist, who arrived in 1911. He is responsible for the Norfolk pines which surround Lanai City, and carried out much resoration work in the highlands, planting trees to protect the eroded hillsides.

Today, only about one-eighth of the island is under pineapple cultivation, but Lanai City, the commercial hub of the island, remains a plantation town. There are only about 40km (25 miles) of sealed roads on Lanai, but there are plenty of hiking trails to take you to remote beaches and incredible mountain scenery.

Lanai is the least visited of all the inhabited islands, and most people who do visit, are day-trippers. At present there are plans for a couple of huge resorts to be built on the island, which will bring much-needed jobs and dollars, but will change the lives of the local inhabitants forever.

HOW TO GET THERE

Hawaiian Airlines has flights to and from Honolulu every day except Saturday. The flight takes about 25 minutes. Air Molokai also have frequent daily flights, as does Aloha Island Air from the other islands.

If you have any heavy gear, it has to be checked in two days before you fly, because it will be shipped on a space available basis.

TOURIST INFORMATION

The Hawaii Visitors' Bureau does not have an office on Lanai.

ACCOMMODATION

As mentioned most people visit Lanai on a day trip from one of the other islands, so there is not much in the way of accommodation until the new resorts are finished.

Bed and Breakfast Hawaii, P.O. Box 449, Kapaa, Kauai, ph 822 7771, can arrange this type of accommodation for $35–55 per person per night, twin share.

The Hotel Lanai, P.O. Box A–119, Lanai, ph 565 7211, is the only hotel on the island at the moment, and its rates range from $51 to $65.

You could also try Four Star Services of Hawaii, 310 Lower Market Street, Wailuku, Maui, ph 527 7819. They have vacation homes available, but not too many.

There is a small camping group at Hulopoe Beach, and for information on this write to the owners, Koele Company, P.O. Box L, Lanai.

LOCAL TRANSPORT

No go here, too. The only car rental companies are Lanai City
Service, ph 565 6780 and Oshiro U-Drive and Taxi, ph 565 6952.

Oshiro also rent jeeps, which considering the road conditions on
the island, are the solution, unless you are very keen on hiking.

To find about road conditions contact Lanai City Service Inc,
ph 565 6780.

EATING OUT

The Hotel Lanai offers three meals a day, and that is it. Breakfast
and lunch are also available at S & T Properties, ph 565 6537, and
Dahang's Bakery, ph 565 6363.

SHOPPING

Richard's Shopping Centre, ph 565 6047, International Food and
Clothing Center, ph 565 6433, and Pine Isle Market, ph 565 6488,
will be able to supply you with anything you have forgotten in the
way of food or toiletries, but not much else.

SIGHTSEEING

One thing to remember when you set out for a trip is that this is a
very dry island, the rainfall being only 1066mm (42″) a year in
the central plain, and the water on the trails is not drinkable, so
make sure you take bottled water with you.

Lanai City
City by name, but really a plantation town built by Dole to house
immigrant labour. It could never be described as a picturesque
village, but it is where all roads on the island lead from (or to). The
town is situated on a level plateau 488m (1,600 ft) above sea level,
below the slope of Lanaihale Mountain (1,027m — 3,370 ft).

Route 44 travels north from Lanai City through arid country
with scrub growth and red soil, but with sweeping views of Maui
and Molokai.

NORTH-EAST AREA

Shipwreck Beach

The strong trade winds between Maui and Molokai have driven many ships on to Lanai's reefs, and the wreck on the beach is a World War II Liberty Ship. There are no facilities on the beach, but the swimming is protected by the reef 200m off shore. To get to the beach take a left turn off Route 44 just before the tar ends, and follow this past squatters' shacks.

There are ancient petroglyphs of simple island scenes at the end of the track, and if you are interested, it is possible to hike from here to Polihua Beach along the shoreline.

Keomuku

Situated on the north-east shore Keomuku is a ghost town 29km (18 miles) from Lanai City. The town was deserted when the Maunalei Sugar Company failed in 1901. The Kahea Heiau is 2.4km (1.5 miles) further on. It appears that stones from this temple were used in the construction of the sugar plantation, and the Hawaiians were convinced that this was the reason for the sugar company's collapse.

The Munro Trail

The Trail, which it must be said is only for the adventurous, begins in Koele off Route 44, about 1.6km (1 mile) north of Lanai City. It is named after George Munro, the New Zealand naturalist, and follows a 11km (7 miles) jeep trail to Lanaihale (1,027m — 3,370 ft), the highest point on Lanai, from where there are views of every Hawaiian island except Kauai.

Hookio Gulch is roughly 3km (2 miles) up the trail, and the ridge beyond is scarred with notches made in 1778 by defending warriors in a futile attempt to defend Lanai against invaders from the Big Island. Close by a path leads to a lookout over Hauola Gulch, the deepest canyon on Lanai (610m —2,000 ft).

The return journey from Lanaihale is either a descent to Hoike Road linking up with Route 441, or by retracing the outward route.

SOUTH-EAST AREA

Luahiwa Petroglyphs

These are not easy to find, but as they are probably the finest rock carvings in Hawaii, they are worth the trouble. They are about

2km (1 mile) from Lanai City off Route 411, through a pineapple field and up a steep cliff, so as you can see it's better to get explicit directions from your hotel.

The clusters of rocks are like a picture gallery, and tell interesting tales of the ancient islanders.

Manele Bay
A small boat harbour containing ruins of old Hawaiian houses, and a park for picnics. There are usually a few sailboats in the bay, and plenty of people around. It is also possible to get a good view of Haleakala on Maui.

Hulopoe Beach
The best beach on Lanai, with a picnic area, showers, rest-rooms, camping facilities, and great swimming, surfing and snorkelling. It's about 13km (8 miles) from Lanai City.

SOUTH-WEST AREA
Kaumalapau Harbour
Route 44 from Lanai City to Kaumalapau Harbour has the most traffic of any road on the island, for it is from this harbour that the pineapples are shipped to Honolulu.

Kaunolu Village
A national landmark, the area was a favourite summer residence of Kamehameha the Great, and his house, which was on the eastern ridge, had views of Halulu Heiau on the opposite side of Kaunolu Bay. This is regarded as the most complete archaeological site in Hawaii, and still has ruins of over eighty houses, stone shelters and graves.

Kahekili's Leap
Quite close to the village is the point from where Kamehameha's warriors tested their strength and courage by diving over 18m (60 ft) to the 4m (12 ft) deep water below, avoiding a 4.5m (15 ft) ledge on the way down. Those who survived were considered fit to be soldiers of such a great king.

NORTH-WEST AREA
Garden of the Gods
On the Awalua Highway, 11km (7 miles) from Lanai City, is the site of unusual lava formations and boulders which change colour

at different times of the day. They look as if they have been placed there by some deity from above.

TOURS

Lanai City Service, P.O. Box N, Lanai City, ph 565 6780, offers tours in 14-seat vans.

Oshiro's Service Station, ph 565 6952, have guided tours ranging from 2 to 4 hours, for a minimum of 2 people.

Alihilani, Lahaina, Maui, ph 661 3047, have a Laina Picnic/Snorkel Sail on a multi-hulled yacht, including lunch, for $39 per person.

Trilogy Excursions, Maui, sail to Lanai on a multi-hulled yacht, including continental breakfast, lunch and guided tour of Lanai, sportfishing, snorkel lessons and gear and swimming at Hulopoe Beach. Leaves Lahaina Harbour at 6.30am, returns about 4.30pm. For reservations ph 661 4743.

SPORT AND RECREATION

Golf
Cavendish Golf Course, Lanai City — 9-holes — green fee $5.

Tennis
Lanai school, ph 565 6464, has two tennis courts.

Hunting
The season for axis deer is from March–May and a licence is required, ph 548 8850.

NIIHAU

Niihau, the Forbidden Isle, is 27km (17 miles) west of Kauai, and has an area of 186km² (72 sq miles). It might just as well be thousands of miles away, because it is privately owned, and until recently visitors were not encouraged. Now the Niihau Ranch has helicopter tours to the island with stops at two remote beaches away from the main town, so are they really worth the effort?

Niihau had its first taste of the western world in 1778, when Captain Cook was anchored off Kauai and his boats were blown over to the shores of Niihau. When he went over to retrieve the boats he bartered some goats, pigs and seeds for salt and vegetables, and so introduced some western animals to the island.

Kamehameha I took control of Kauai in 1810, and Niihau was part of the package. He apparently didn't think much of it because he sold it to Mrs Elizabeth Sinclair, a Scottish widow from New Zealand, for $10,000. Now the island is owned by her great-great-grandsons, Bruce and Keith Robinson, and their mother Helen.

Niihau has its own dialect of Hawaiian, which is the main language, with English being taught as a second language in the school. There is no police force, no cinemas, no telephones, no hospital, no doctor or dentist, no electricity, no water system, and no alcohol. In fact, life is much as it was in the early 1900s, and the islanders want it to stay that way, so in the 1959 vote on Hawaii's statehood, Niihau was the only district to vote against it.

The Robinson Ranch raises cattle and sheep, the sheep coming from the herd that Mrs Sinclair originally brought to the island. They also keep bees, which is proving a money-spinner, producing about 27,216kg (60,000 pounds) per year of kiawe blossom honey. Then there is the Niihau Sunset Brand Charcoal which is also proving a success, with half of its output being shipped to Mainland USA. But with the short, wet winters and long hot summers, the Robinson family is always facing one challenge or another to keep their tiny island solvent, hence the helicopter tours.

About the only thing Niihau is known for, apart from its isolation from the outside world, is its shell jewellery. Niihau shells are found on the other islands, but not in such large numbers, and every day people sift the sands and sort out the burgundy, brown, blue and speckled shells. Leis made from these shells have been known to fetch thousands of dollars.

Residents of the islands are free to leave, to further their education or whatever, but the majority return.

———————————

INDEX

Ahihi-Kinau Reserve (Maui)   103
Ala Moana Park (Oahu)   44
Alaka Falls State Park
   (Hawaii)   74
Alii Drive (Hawaii)   78
Aloha Tower (Oahu)   41
Anahola Beach (Kauai)   133

Banyan Drive (Hawaii)   73
Barking Sands (Kauai)   131
Big Island — see Hawaii
Bird Park (Hawaii)   81
Bishop Museum & Planetarium
   (Oahu)   47
Byodo-In Temple (Oahu)   50

Cape Kumukahi Lighthouse
   (Hawaii)   83
Captain Cook Monument
   (Hawaii)   79
Captain Cook's Landing
   (Kauai)   130
Castle Park (Oahu)   47
Charles Lindbergh's Grave
   (Maui)   106
Coconut Island (Hawaii)   73
Coronation Pavilion (Oahu)   41

Devastation Trail (Hawaii)   81
Diamond Head (Oahu)   46

Fern Grotto (Kauai)   134
Fort DeRussy Army Museum
   (Oahu)   45–46
Fort Elizabeth (Kauai)   130
Foster Botanic Garden
   (Oahu)   44

Garden of the Gods (Lanai)   143
Green Sands Beach (Hawaii)   80

Haiku Gardens (Oahu)   50
Halawa Valley (Molokai)   117
Haleakala National Park
   (Maui)   107
Haleiwa (Oahu)   53
Halekii Heiau (Maui)   101
Halemaumau Crater (Hawaii)   82
Halona Blowhole (Oahu)   49
Hamakua Coast (Hawaii)   74–75
Hamoa Beach (Maui)   106
Hana Bay (Maui)   105
Hanalei Valley (Kauai)   132
Hanapepe (Kauai)   130
Hanauma Bay (Oahu)   48
Hauula Beach Park (Oahu)   50
Hawaii (The Big Island)   61–87
   — Accommodation   63–64
   — Car Rental   65
   — Eating Out and
         Entertainment   66–70
   — How To Get There   61
   — Local Transport   64
   — Shopping   70–73
   — Sightseeing   73–84
   — Sport and
         Recreation   84–87
   — Tourist Information   61
   — Tours   83–84
Hawaiian Islands
   — Climate   15–16
   — Communications   21
   — Embassies   20
   — Entry Regulations   20
   — Festivals   19

— Food   24
— History   8–14
— Language   16–18
— Miscellaneous   21–22
— Money   21
— Official Emblems   14–15
— Population   16
— Religion   18–19
— Shopping   24
— Sport and Recreation   25
— Travel Information   23–25
Hawaii Maritime Centre
   (Oahu)   44
Hikiau Heiau (Hawaii)   79
Hilo (Hawaii)   73–74
Honokaa (Hawaii)   75
Honokohau Bay (Maui)   101
Honolulu (Oahu)   40–48
— Downtown   40–44
— Greater   46–48
— Midtown   44–45
Honolulu Academy of Arts
   (Oahu)   44
Honolulu Zoo (Oahu)   45
Honomanu Bay (Maui)   105
Hulihee Palace & Museum
   (Hawaii)   78
Hulopoe Beach (Lanai)   143

Iao Needle (Maui)   104
Iao Valley (Maui)   104
Iliiliopae Heiau (Molokai)   117
Iolani Barracks (Oahu)   40
Iolani Palace (Oahu)   40

Kaanapali (Maui)   101
Kahakuloa (Maui)   101
Kahekili's Leap (Lanai)   143
Kahuku (Oahu)   51
Kahului (Maui)   103
Kaiae (Molokai)   118
Kailua (Hawaii)   78–79

Kailua (Oahu)   49
Kaimu (Hawaii)   82
Kalakau Lookout (Kauai)   131
Kalalea Heiau (Hawaii)   80
Kalama Country Beach Park
   (Maui)   102
Kalapana (Hawaii)   82
Kalaupapa (Molokai)   119
Kalaupapa Lookout
   (Molokai)   118
Kalopa State Park (Hawaii)   75
Kaluaaha Church (Molokai)   116
Kaluakoi Resort (Molokai)   120
Kamakou (Molokai)   115
Kamaole Beach Parks
   (Maui)   102
Kamokila Hawaiian Village
   (Kauai)   134
Kanaha Pond Wildlife Sanctuary
   (Maui)   103
Kaneana Cave (Oahu)   53
Kaneohe (Oahu)   50
Kapaa Beach (Kauai)   133
Kapaau (Hawaii)   76
Kapalua Beach (Maui)   101
Kapiolani Park (Oahu)   45
Kauai   121–137
— Accommodation   123–125
— Car Rental   125–126
— Eating Out   126–127
— Entertainment   127–128
— How To Get There   121
— Local Transport   125
— Shopping   128–129
— Sightseeing   129–134
— Sport and
      Recreation   135–137
— Tourist Information   123
— Tours   134–135
Kauai, North Shore   132–134
Kauai, South Shore   130–131
Kauluwai (Molokai)   118

Kaumalapau Harbour
(Lanai) 143
Kaumana Caves (Hawaii) 74
Kaunakakai (Molokai) 114–115
Kaunolu Village (Lanai) 143
Kaupo (Maui) 106
Kawaiahao Church (Oahu) 41
Kawela (Molokai) 115
Kealia Beach (Kauai) 133
Keanae Arboretum (Maui) 105
Keauhou Bay (Hawaii) 79
Keawenui Fishpond
(Molokai) 116
Ke'e Beach (Kauai) 132
Keomuku (Lanai) 142
Kewalo Boat Basin (Oahu) 45
Kihei Beach (Maui) 102
Kilauea Iki Trail (Hawaii) 81
Kilauea Lighthouse (Kauai) 132
King Kamehameha Statue
(Oahu) 41
Kohala Coast (Hawaii) 76–78
Kohala Mountains (Hawaii) 76
Kokee Park (Kauai) 131
Koloa (Kauai) 130
Kona Historical Society Museum
(Hawaii) 79
Kona, South (Hawaii) 79–80
Kualapuu (Molokai) 118
Kualoa Regional Park (Oahu) 50
Kulu Botanical Gardens
(Maui) 106

Lahaina (Maui) 99–100
Laie (Oahu) 51
Lanai 139–144
— Accommodation 140
— Car Rental 141
— How To Get There 140
— Local Transport 141
— Shopping 141
— Sightseeing 141–144

— Sport and Recreation 144
— Tourist Information 140
— Tours 144
Lanai, North-East Area 142
Lanai, North-West
Area 143–144
Lanai, South-East Area 142–143
Lanai, South-West Area 143
Lanai City (Lanai) 141
Lanikaula Grove (Molokai) 117
Lapakahi State Historical Park
(Hawaii) 76
La Perouse Bay (Maui) 103
Launiupoko State Park
(Maui) 99
Laupahoehoe Point (Hawaii) 75
Lihue (Kauai) 129 —130
Liliuokalani Church (Oahu) 53
Liliuokalani Gardens Park
(Hawaii) 73
Luahiwa Petroglyphs
(Lanai) 142
Lumahai Beach (Kauai) 132
Lyman House Memorial Museum
(Hawaii) 74

Maalaea Bay (Maui) 102
Makaha (Oahu) 54
Makapuu Beach (Oahu) 49
Makawao (Maui) 107
Makena (Maui) 103
Mana (Kauai) 131
Manele Bay (Lanai) 143
Manoa Valley (Oahu) 48
Maui 89–110
— Accommodation 90–93
— Car Rental 94
— Eating Out 95–97
— Entertainment 97
— How To Get There 89
— Local Transport 93–94
— Shopping 98–99

— Sightseeing 99–110
— Snorkelling, Diving,
    Sailing 107–109
— Tourist Information 89
— Tours 109–110
Maui, Central 103–104
Maui, East 104–107
Maui, South 102–103
Maui, West 99–101
Maunaloa (Molokai) 120
Menehune Ditch (Kauai) 131
Mililani (Oahu) 55
Mission Houses Museum
  (Oahu) 41
Moanui Sugar Mill
  (Molokai) 117
Mokuaikaua Church (Hawaii) 78
Mokuleia (Oahu) 53
Moloaa Beach (Kauai) 133
Molokai 111–120
— Accommodation 113
— Car Rental 113
— Eating Out 113–114
— Entertainment 114
— How To Get There 111
— Local Transport 113
— Shopping 114
— Sightseeing 114–120
— Sport and Recreation 120
— Tourist Information 111
— Tours
Molokai Ranch Wildlife Park
  (Molokai) 119
Mookini Heiau (Hawaii) 76
Munro Trail (Lanai) 142

Naalehu (Hawaii) 81
Naha Stone (Hawaii) 74
Napili (Maui) 101
Niihau 145–146
Nuuanu Pali Lookout (Oahu) 47
Nuu Landing (Maui) 106

Oahu 27–60
— Accommodation 28–30
— Car Rental 33–34
— Eating Out 34–36
— Entertainment 36–38
— How To Get There 27–28
— Local Transport 31–33
— Package Tours 30–31
— Shopping 38–40
— Sightseeing 40–55
— Sport & Recreation 58–60
— Tourist Information 28
— Tours 55–58
Oahu, Central 54–55
Oahu, North Shore 51–53
Oahu, South-East 48–49
Oahu, Western 53–54
Windward 49–51
Octopus Stone (Molokai) 116
Olowahu Beaches (Maui) 99
One Alii Park (Molokai) 115
Opaekaa Falls (Kauai) 133
Our Lady of Sorrows Church
  (Molokai) 116

Paauilo (Hawaii) 75
Paia (Maui) 104
Palaau Park (Molokai) 118
Palahemo Well (Hawaii) 80
Pali Coastline (Molokai) 119
Pearl Harbour (Oahu) 46–47
Phallic Rock (Molokai) 118
Poipu Beach (Kauai) 130
Pokai Bay Beach Park (Oahu) 54
Polynesian Cultural Center
  (Oahu) 51
Puaa Kaa State Park (Maui) 105
Puako Petroglyphs (Hawaii) 78
Puamana Park (Maui) 99
Puna (Hawaii) 82–83
Punchbowl (Oahu) 48
Puohokamoa Falls (Maui) 104

Pupukea Beach Park (Oahu) 52
Pu'uhonua O Honaunau
  (Hawaii) 79
Puukohola Heiau (Hawaii) 78
Puu Kukui (Maui) 101
Puu Mano (Molokai) 117
Puu O Hoku Ranch
  (Molokai) 117
Puu O Mahuka Heiau (Oahu) 52

Queen Emma's Summer Palace
  (Oahu) 47
Queen Victoria's Profile
  (Kauai) 130

Rabbit Island (Oahu) 49
Rainbow Falls (Hawaii) 74
Royal Birth Stones (Kauai) 133

Sacred Falls (Oahu) 50
St Andrew's Cathedral
  (Oahu) 41
St Benedict's Church
  (Hawaii) 80
St Joseph's Church
  (Molokai) 115
St Peter's Catholic Church
  (Hawaii) 79
Sandalwood Pit (Molokai) 118
Schofield Barracks (Oahu) 55
Sea Life Park (Oahu) 49
Shipwreck Beach (Lanai) 142
Sleeping Giant (Kauai) 133
Smith & Bronte Landing
  (Molokai) 115
Smith's Tropical Paradise
  (Kauai) 133
South Point (Hawaii) 80–82
Spouting Horn (Kauai) 130
Star of the Sea Painted Church
  (Hawaii) 82
State Capital (Oahu) 41
Suisan Fish Auction (Hawaii) 73
Sunset Beach (Oahu) 51

Twin Falls (Maui) 104

Ualapue Fishpond
  (Molokai) 116
Ulupalakua Ranch (Maui) 106

Volcanoes National Park
  (Hawaii) 81
Volcano Village (Hawaii) 82

Wahau'la Park (Hawaii) 82
Wahiawa (Oahu) 54–55
Wahikuli State Park (Maui) 100
Waianapanapa State Park
  (Maui) 105
Waikiki (Oahu) 45–46
Waikiki Aquarium (Oahu) 45
Waikolu Valley (Molokai) 118
Wailau Trail (Molokai) 117
Wailea (Maui) 102
Wailoa River & State Park
  (Hawaii) 73
Wailua (Maui) 105
Wailua (Molokai) 117
Wailua Gulch (Maui) 106
Wailuku (Maui) 103
Waimanalo Beach (Oahu) 49
Waimea (Hawaii) 76–78
Waimea Bay (Oahu) 52
Waimea Canyon (Kauai) 131
Waimea Falls Park (Oahu) 52
Waiohinu (Hawaii) 81
Waioli Mission House
  (Kauai) 132
Waipi'o Valley (Hawaii) 75
Wakefield Botanical Gardens
  (Hawaii) 80
Washington Place (Oahu) 41
Wet & Dry Caves (Kauai) 132
Whittington Beach Park
  (Hawaii) 81

Yokohama Bay Beach (Oahu) 53